Lee Canter's

Assertive Discipline®
Elementary Workbook

Grades K-5

A Publication of Lee Canter & Associates

Staff Writer
Marcia Shank

Editorial Staff
Marlene Canter
Jacqui Hook
Patricia Sarka
Kathy Winberry

Design
Bob Winberry

Illustrations
Jane Yamada
Patty Briles

P.O. Box 2113, Santa Monica, CA 90407-2113
800-262-4347 310-395-3221

Printed in the United States of America
First printing May 1992

96 95 94 11 10 9 8 7 6 5 4

ISBN 0-939007-48-7

Contents

Introduction

Lee Canter's Assertive Discipline has been a highly regarded classroom behavior management program for over 15 years. In 1992 the program was revised to more comprehensively meet the needs of today's classrooms. The focus of the new Assertive Discipline is on teaching students responsible behavior. With this proactive and preventive approach, teachers can go beyond establishing basic discipline in their classrooms to creating learning environments in which students learn to choose appropriate, responsible behavior.

This *Assertive Discipline Elementary Workbook* is your guide to implementing the revised Assertive Discipline program. The easy-to-follow format is concise and comfortable. Brief overviews of the program's key points are followed by the reproducible forms, positive notes, awards, badges, bookmarks, coupons, tracking sheets, communication and documentation pages, and visual aids that will allow you to successfully integrate the program into your teaching routine.

For a comprehensive understanding of the revised Assertive Discipline program, please read *Assertive Discipline—Positive Behavior Management for Today's Classroom.*

Positive Classroom Behavior Management and the Elementary Classroom

Being an elementary teacher is a challenging job—especially in today's world. You may find, like many teachers today, that it is increasingly difficult to establish a classroom environment free from disruptive behavior.

But in spite of the difficulties you face, you *can* create and maintain the kind of classroom in which you can effectively teach and your students can learn and grow academically and socially.

How can you achieve this? By becoming an assertive teacher—an empowered teacher—a teacher of influence. Whatever the age of your students, they will behave more responsibly and have more success at school if you follow these guidelines:

- Establish rules and specific directions that clearly define the limits of acceptable and unacceptable student behavior.
- Teach your students to consistently follow these rules and directions—to choose to behave responsibly—throughout the school day and the school year.
- Provide students with consistent positive encouragement and recognition when they do behave. All children are eager for your positive words of encouragement and praise.
- Adopt a positive, assertive manner when responding to students. Young students trust and respect the calm, consistent and caring presence of an assertive teacher. They know that the teacher has set limits and that he or she will follow through appropriately whenever a student chooses not to behave. There is no confusion, no second guessing, no hostility or anger.
- Remember to ask parents and administrators for their assistance when their support is needed. You can't do it alone. Education is a cooperative effort between teacher, student, parents and administration. Rely on each other for the positive assistance you can give.

Make the most of these formative years in elementary school. Create an atmosphere in which student self-esteem can flourish and you can feel accomplished at the end of every teaching day. Become a positive, proactive, assertive teacher—today!

SECTION ONE

Your Classroom Discipline Plan

In this section of the Assertive Discipline Elementary Workbook we will first look at the classroom discipline plan—what it is and what it can do for you and your students. Then you will develop a discipline plan for your own classroom with rules, positives and consequences that best fit your needs, and the needs of your students.

Also included in this section are a wide variety of reproducibles that will help you successfully develop and implement your classroom discipline plan.

What Is a Classroom Discipline Plan?

A classroom discipline plan is a system that allows you to spell out the behaviors you expect from students and what they can expect from you in return. The plan provides a framework around which all of your classroom behavior management efforts can be organized.

The goal of a classroom discipline plan is to have a fair and consistent way to establish a safe, orderly, positive classroom environment in which you can teach and students can learn.

A classroom discipline plan consists of three parts:

- RULES that students must follow at all times.
- POSITIVE RECOGNITION that students will receive for following the rules.
- CONSEQUENCES that result when students choose not to follow the rules.

Here's a sample classroom discipline plan for an elementary classroom:

CLASSROOM RULES

Follow directions.
Keep hands, feet and objects to yourself.
No teasing or name calling.

POSITIVE RECOGNITION

Praise
First in line for recess
Positive notes sent home to parents
Positive notes to students
Eat lunch with teacher
Select own seat on Friday

CONSEQUENCES

First time a student breaks a rule:	Warning
Second time:	5 minutes working away from group
Third time:	10 minutes working away from group
Fourth time:	Teacher calls parents
Fifth time:	Send to principal
Severe Clause:	Send to principal

Benefits of a Classroom Discipline Plan

Here are four reasons why a classroom discipline plan will help you create a learning environment in your classroom that benefits both you and your students.

1 A discipline plan makes managing student behavior easier.

Planning is the key to successful classroom management. When you have a plan for how you will respond to student behavior you won't have to make on-the-spot decisions about what to do when a student misbehaves—or how to properly recognize a student who does behave appropriately. You'll know what to do, your students will know what to expect, and the guesswork (and stress) will be eliminated from your daily disciplinary efforts.

2 A discipline plan protects students' rights.

All students have the right to the same due process in the classroom. A discipline plan will help ensure that you deal with each student in a fair and consistent manner.

3 A discipline plan helps ensure parental support.

When you communicate your discipline plan to parents, (see pages 72-74) you are letting them know that you care about teaching their children to behave responsibly. This is a powerful message of support and professionalism to give to parents.

4 A discipline plan helps ensure administrator support.

A discipline plan demonstrates to your administrator that you have a well-thought-out course of action for managing student behavior in your classroom. When your administrator understands the commitment you've made to effective classroom management, you will be better able to get support when you need it.

It's Your Turn

Now we'll take you through the steps of creating a classroom discipline plan tailor-made for you and your students.

First, you will plan the general rules for your classroom.

Second, you will choose the positive recognition you will use to motivate students to follow those rules.

Finally, you will learn how to most effectively select and use consequences when students choose not to follow the rules.

Creating Your Classroom Discipline Plan

Rules

Whether kindergarteners or sixth-graders, your students all share something in common when they arrive in your classroom—each brings a variety of behavioral expectations from home and a variety of behavioral expectations from previous teachers.

These expectations, however, may not be *your* behavioral expectations.

Your students can't be expected to know how you want them to behave in your classroom unless you make those expectations clear to them. General classroom rules, therefore, are the first part of your classroom discipline plan.

What are general classroom rules?

General classroom rules are those rules that are in place all day long—throughout all activities. General classroom rules are important because they let your students know what basic behavioral expectations you have.

These guidelines will help you choose appropriate classroom rules:

- **Choose rules that are observable.**

Address behaviors that you can clearly see. Vaguely stated expectations may mean one thing to one child, and an entirely different thing to another. As a result, they often cause problems by opening the door to arguments.

For example:

Observable Rules

Keep hands and feet to yourself.

Be in line when the bell rings.

No yelling or screaming.

Vague Expectations

Be kind to other students.

No fooling around when class starts.

No unnecessary talking.

- **Choose rules that apply throughout the entire day.**

General classroom rules are rules that apply all day, no matter what activity is taking place. These are rules that students are expected to follow at all times.

Now, before you choose your own rules, take a look on the next page at some rules that are *not* appropriate general classroom rules. Though often seen in classrooms, we have found that these rules are not appropriate general classroom rules because they are not applicable throughout the entire day. Notice that while each rule *sounds* sensible, it cannot be a realistic ongoing expectation.

Rules to Avoid:

- Raise your hand and wait to be called upon before you speak.

There are going to be times when students are expected to speak out (for example, in cooperative learning groups). Therefore, this is not an appropriate general classroom rule.

- Stay in your seat unless you have permission to get up.

There may be many times during the day when it's OK for a student to get up without asking permission. Again, this rule will not be enforceable throughout the day.

- Use a 12-inch voice in the classroom.

Of course there will be times when students need to speak up! Do not make voice-level requirements part of your general classroom rules.

- Complete all homework assignments.

This rule does not relate to classroom behavior. Also, there may be times when completing homework is out of a student's control.

When you establish general classroom rules that do not clearly reflect your consistent expectations, you run the risk of confusing students, and you will not be able to enforce these rules with consistency.

Here are some general classroom rules that are appropriate for grades K-5.

Notice that each of these rules is applicable throughout the entire day and that each one is observable.

- Follow directions.
- Keep hands, feet and objects to yourself.
- Do not leave the room without permission.
- No swearing or teasing.
- No yelling or screaming.
- Use appropriate school language

It's Your Turn

Use the Classroom Rules Worksheet on the next page to plan the general classroom rules you will use in your own classroom. When you're finished, write your rules on the Classroom Rules poster on pages 11-12.

CLASSROOM RULES WORKSHEET

Use this worksheet to plan your own general classroom rules. We've started the list for you with the rule, "Follow directions." This is an important rule because students must be expected to follow any direction you might give during the day. When choosing the rest of your rules, remember: 1) Rules must be observable, and 2) Rules must apply throughout the entire day.

Classroom Rule: Follow directions.

This is an appropriate general classroom rule because:

____

____

____

____

Classroom Rule: ______________________________

This is an appropriate general classroom rule because:

____

____

____

____

Classroom Rule: ______________________________

This is an appropriate general classroom rule because:

____

____

____

____

Classroom Rule: ______________________________

This is an appropriate general classroom rule because:

____

____

____

____

OUR CLASSROOM RULES!

Creating Your Classroom Discipline Plan
Positive Recognition

Your general classroom rules are the first part of your classroom discipline plan. The second part of your discipline plan, positive recognition, will help you motivate your students to follow these rules.

Positive recognition is the sincere and meaningful attention you give a student for behaving according to your expectations.

Positive recognition is a powerful motivator for elementary-age students. Consistently used, positive recognition will:

- Encourage your students to behave appropriately.
- Increase your students' self-esteem.
- Dramatically reduce problem behaviors.
- Create a positive classroom climate for you and your students.
- Help you teach behavior and establish positive relationships with your students.

Refer to pages 57-62 of the revised Assertive Discipline text for an in-depth look at these benefits of positive recognition.

With these benefits in mind, let's take a look now at five ways you can provide positive recognition to individual students:

1 Praise

2 Positive notes and phone calls home

3 Special privileges

4 Behavior awards

5 Tangible rewards

Praise (Analytical Feedback)

You know that elementary-age students enjoy receiving positive recognition from their teacher. An award, sticker or special treat is always welcomed and appreciated. But did you know that the most meaningful and effective means of positive recognition you can give are your own words of praise?

When you take the time to say something positive about a student's achievement, you are making a statement that will have a long-lasting impact. You are saying, "I care about you. I notice the good work you are doing and I'm proud of you."

Praise should be your #1 choice in positive recognition.

To make the praise you give as effective as possible, keep these guidelines in mind:

- **Effective praise is personal.**

Maximize the impact of praise by including the student's name in your comments, and watch the smiles appear and self-esteem soar!

> "Maria, thank you for working so cooperatively with Lauren in your group."

- **Effective praise must be genuine.**

Children recognize sincere words when they hear them. Make sure your words of praise genuinely reflect your own feelings of pride in a student's accomplishments.

- **Effective praise is descriptive and specific.**

Praise will be most effective when it refers to something specific the student has accomplished. "I am so proud of the way you helped tutor the first-graders today, Samantha," sounds much more meaningful than, "Great job, Samantha."

It's Your Turn

Start thinking now about all of the opportunities you have each day to verbally recognize your students' successes—all of the moments when an admiring word from you can make a big difference in a student's life. Jot notes in your plan book reminding yourself to look for students' good behavior, then say something about it!

Timely reminders.
As an extra reminder to consistently praise students, make a copy of the "The Time Is Right for Super Classroom Behavior" poster on page 15. Hang this reminder on the classroom wall right next to the clock. This timely note will give you a nudge throughout the day to keep looking for positive behavior to reinforce.

Looking for just the right moment to say "good for you?"
There are hundreds of opportunities to praise students each day of the year. Don't let these moments slip by. To help you further develop the praise habit, we've put together a list of 50 Opportunities to say "You're Terrific" (page 16). Keep this sheet in your desk or plan book and review it from time to time as a reminder of all the occasions throughout the school day in which you can verbally recognize a student's good behavior.

50 OPPORTUNITIES TO SAY "YOU'RE TERRIFIC"

Praise students for:

1. entering the classroom quietly
2. putting away coat and backpack
3. cooperating while teacher takes attendance
4. returning permission slips and school forms on time
5. transitioning into an activity
6. following directions
7. saying "please," and "thank you"
8. listening attentively
9. helping a classmate
10. lining up
11. handing in homework
12. being a good audience at an assembly
13. beginning work right away
14. asking questions when unsure
15. good behavior during a test
16. participating in a class discussion
17. walking appropriately in the halls
18. working cooperatively with a partner
19. good behavior during a field trip
20. cleaning up
21. good effort on an assignment
22. assisting a new student
23. sharing school experiences with parents
24. making up missed assignments
25. making a new friend
26. good effort on a long-term project
27. sharing
28. being sensitive to others' feelings
29. learning a new skill
30. appropriate use of school property
31. returning borrowed books and materials
32. showing enthusiasm
33. being responsible for a classroom job
34. offering help without being asked
35. not wasting paper and supplies
36. staying on task
37. telling the truth
38. accepting a new challenge
39. behaving when a guest is in the room
40. reading at home
41. participating in school functions
42. demonstrating a positive attitude
43. giving one's best effort
44. returning from the yard quietly
45. participating in a group activity
46. remaining calm during a problem situation
47. showing creativity
48. keeping busy when work is finished
49. taking turns
50. working cooperatively with an aide or volunteer

The time is right
for super
classroom
behavior!
1
2
3
4
5
© Lee Canter & Associates

50 OPPORTUNITIES TO SAY "YOU'RE TERRIFIC"

Praise students for:

1. entering the classroom quietly
2. putting away coat and backpack
3. cooperating while teacher takes attendance
4. returning permission slips and school forms on time
5. transitioning into an activity
6. following directions
7. saying "please," and "thank you"
8. listening attentively
9. helping a classmate
10. lining up
11. handing in homework
12. being a good audience at an assembly
13. beginning work right away
14. asking questions when unsure
15. good behavior during a test
16. participating in a class discussion
17. walking appropriately in the halls
18. working cooperatively with a partner
19. good behavior during a field trip
20. cleaning up
21. good effort on an assignment
22. assisting a new student
23. sharing school experiences with parents
24. making up missed assignments
25. making a new friend
26. good effort on a long-term project
27. sharing
28. being sensitive to others' feelings
29. learning a new skill
30. appropriate use of school property
31. returning borrowed books and materials
32. showing enthusiasm
33. being responsible for a classroom job
34. offering help without being asked
35. not wasting paper and supplies
36. staying on task
37. telling the truth
38. accepting a new challenge
39. behaving when a guest is in the room
40. reading at home
41. participating in school functions
42. demonstrating a positive attitude
43. giving one's best effort
44. returning from the yard quietly
45. participating in a group activity
46. remaining calm during a problem situation
47. showing creativity
48. keeping busy when work is finished
49. taking turns
50. working cooperatively with an aide or volunteer

Positive Notes and Phone Calls

Good news in the mail or via the phone is always welcomed! It makes sense, then, that positive notes and phone calls be an important part of your positive recognition planning.

The goal of a positive note or phone call is to share with parents "good news" about their child. Telling your students that you will send positive messages to parents about their good behavior is a great motivator. Few things are as important to children as knowing their parents are proud of them and the work they are doing.

It's also a great way to establish a positive relationship with parents. Throughout the year you will need parental support. It will be much easier to gain that support when you need it if you have already begun building a positive foundation.

Positive phone calls and notes don't take much time, but they pay big dividends.

Here's what a positive phone call to a parent might sound like:

> "Mrs. Smith? This is Miss Walker, Jonathan's teacher. I want you to know that Jonathan is making a great start at school this year. This first week we've spent a lot of time learning to follow the classroom rules, and I'm happy to let you know that Jonathan is following those rules and setting a great example for the other students.
>
> "Please tell Jonathan that I called and how pleased I am with his behavior in class."

Just that easy and just that quick. In a few brief moments this teacher has established a positive relationship with a parent and boosted the self-esteem of a student.

And here's what a positive note might say:

Dear Mr. and Mrs. Washington,

I am so pleased to let you know what a wonderful job Elise is doing in my class. She listens when directions are given, and follows the directions quickly and quietly. That's very important when you're in a room with 30 children! This kind of responsible behavior will help Elise do a good job in her schoolwork. You should be very proud of the effort she's making.

Sincerely,

Mrs. Smith

It's Your Turn

Once you recognize how easy it really is to make positive contact with parents, you'll be convinced that it's an effective use of your time. The suggestions that follow will help you develop this positive parent involvement habit.

First, set goals!

Set a goal to make a specific number of positive phone calls and to send a specific number of positive notes home each week. (Just two contacts a day will guarantee that you reach each and every parent with good news each month!) To make sure that all students receive this important attention, keep track of your positive contacts on the Positive Parent Communication Log on page 19.

Next, remember the good things that happen!

Use the Positive Memos on page 20 to jot down positive comments you want to remember and later share with parents in a note or phone call. Run off copies of the memos and keep a stack close by in your desk. During the day when something "memo"rable happens that you'd like to communicate, write it down! You may wish to keep this memo as part of a student's documentation file.

Finally, be sure to share the good news!

Use the reproducible positive notes on pages 21-22 any time you want parents and students to know how proud you are of a student's achievement. Run off copies of these reproducible notes, keep them handy, and use them frequently! (Keep track of notes home on the Positive Parent Communication Log.)

POSITIVE PARENT COMMUNICATION LOG

Use this sheet to keep track of your positive communication efforts by circling N for note, PC for phone call and O for other.

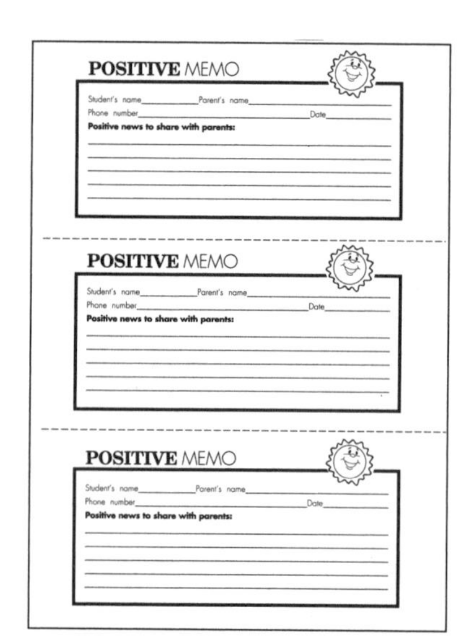

POSITIVE MEMO

Student's name ______ Parent's name ______
Phone number ______ Date ______
Positive news to share with parents:

POSITIVE MEMO

Student's name ______ Parent's name ______
Phone number ______ Date ______
Positive news to share with parents:

POSITIVE MEMO

Student's name ______ Parent's name ______
Phone number ______ Date ______
Positive news to share with parents:

POSITIVE PARENT COMMUNICATION LOG

Use this sheet to keep track of your positive communication efforts by circling N for note, PC for phone call and O for other.

Student	**Month of**	**Month of**	**Month of**	**Month of**	**Month of**	**Month of**
	N PC O	N PC O	N PC O	N PC O	N PC O	N PC O
	N PC O	N PC O	N PC O	N PC O	N PC O	N PC O
	N PC O	N PC O	N PC O	N PC O	N PC O	N PC O
	N PC O	N PC O	N PC O	N PC O	N PC O	N PC O
	N PC O	N PC O	N PC O	N PC O	N PC O	N PC O
	N PC O	N PC O	N PC O	N PC O	N PC O	N PC O
	N PC O	N PC O	N PC O	N PC O	N PC O	N PC O
	N PC O	N PC O	N PC O	N PC O	N PC O	N PC O
	N PC O	N PC O	N PC O	N PC O	N PC O	N PC O
	N PC O	N PC O	N PC O	N PC O	N PC O	N PC O
	N PC O	N PC O	N PC O	N PC O	N PC O	N PC O
	N PC O	N PC O	N PC O	N PC O	N PC O	N PC O
	N PC O	N PC O	N PC O	N PC O	N PC O	N PC O
	N PC O	N PC O	N PC O	N PC O	N PC O	N PC O
	N PC O	N PC O	N PC O	N PC O	N PC O	N PC O
	N PC O	N PC O	N PC O	N PC O	N PC O	N PC O
	N PC O	N PC O	N PC O	N PC O	N PC O	N PC O
	N PC O	N PC O	N PC O	N PC O	N PC O	N PC O
	N PC O	N PC O	N PC O	N PC O	N PC O	N PC O
	N PC O	N PC O	N PC O	N PC O	N PC O	N PC O
	N PC O	N PC O	N PC O	N PC O	N PC O	N PC O
	N PC O	N PC O	N PC O	N PC O	N PC O	N PC O

POSITIVE MEMO

Student's name__________ Parent's name__________

Phone number__________ Date__________

Positive news to share with parents:

POSITIVE MEMO

Student's name__________ Parent's name__________

Phone number__________ Date__________

Positive news to share with parents:

POSITIVE MEMO

Student's name__________ Parent's name__________

Phone number__________ Date__________

Positive news to share with parents:

Great News to Share!
© Lee Canter & Associates

Student's name
deserves a big hand
for
Signed
Date
© Lee Canter & Associates

Signed

Date

Time to share some GOOD NEWS!

Signed

Date

Behavior Awards

Special awards for good behavior are always a great motivator for elementary-age students because they have a double impact!

1 Students will be proud to receive them from you, and

2 they'll be proud to take them home to show to parents!

Tell students that one way you'll recognize good behavior throughout the year is by sending home special awards that let them and their parents know how responsibly they are behaving in school.

To keep yourself on track, plan to send home a specific number of awards each week.

It's Your Turn

On the following pages you will find a variety of behavior awards designed especially for elementary students.

- Primary students will enjoy receiving the "good behavior" badges and bookmarks on pages 24 and 25.
- Upper elementary students will appreciate the bookmarks on page 26.
- All students, and their parents, will appreciate the behavior certificates (pages 27-31)—certificates that are sure to be proudly displayed at home and later kept in scrapbooks. Just fill in the good behavior you want to recognize and present the award to the deserving student!

FLYING HIGH WITH
GOOD BEHAVIOR!!!
HEARTFELT THANKS FOR
GOOD BEHAVIOR
GOOD BEHAVIOR
MAKES YOU A STAR!

's
Student's name
behavior is
"purr-fectly"
wonderful.
Thanks!
Signed
Date
© Lee Canter & Associates

A little
mouse told
me that
Student's name
always
follows
directions.
Thanks!
Signed
Date
© Lee Canter & Associates

To: ______________________
Student's name

You're in Great Shape with Great Behavior!

Keep up the good work!

SUPERSTAR
© Lee Canter & Associates

THERE'S
NO
END
TO
GOOD
BEHAVIOR

Student's name
gets "high marks" for improved behavior because
Great job!
Signed
Date
© Lee Canter & Associates

Your "royal" behavior is noticed because
Signed
Date

Your super behavior,
Student's name
is music to
my ears!
Thanks!
Signed
Date
© Lee Canter & Associates

To:
Student's name
If you're fishing for
compliments, just
let me say,
your behavior was
positively perfect today!
SUPER
BEHAVIOR
Signed
Date
© Lee Canter & Associates

Certificate of
Super Behavior
Presented to
For
Teacher's Signature
Date
© Lee Canter & Associates

Any way you "slice it",

______________________________'s
Student's name

behavior is delightful!

Thank you for

____
____
____
____
____

____
Signed Date

- -

To: ______________________________
Student's name

Your terrific behavior helps make our class special.

Thank you for

____
____
____

____
Signed Date

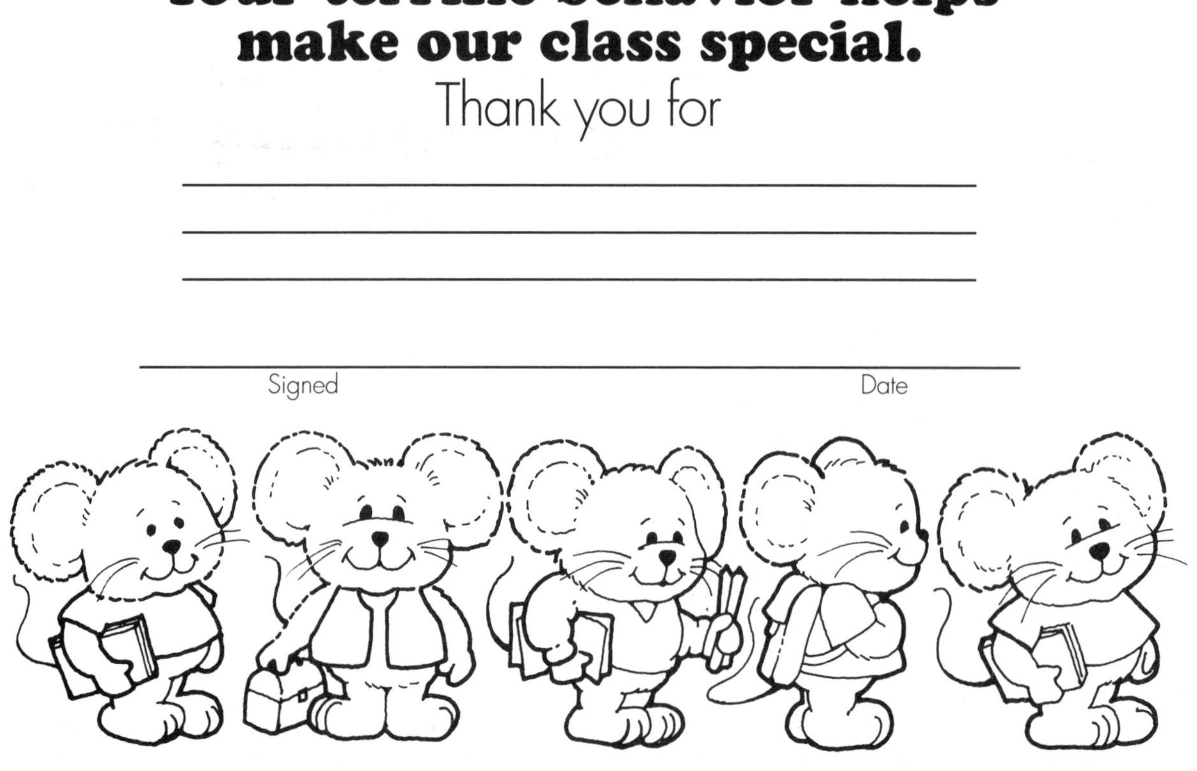

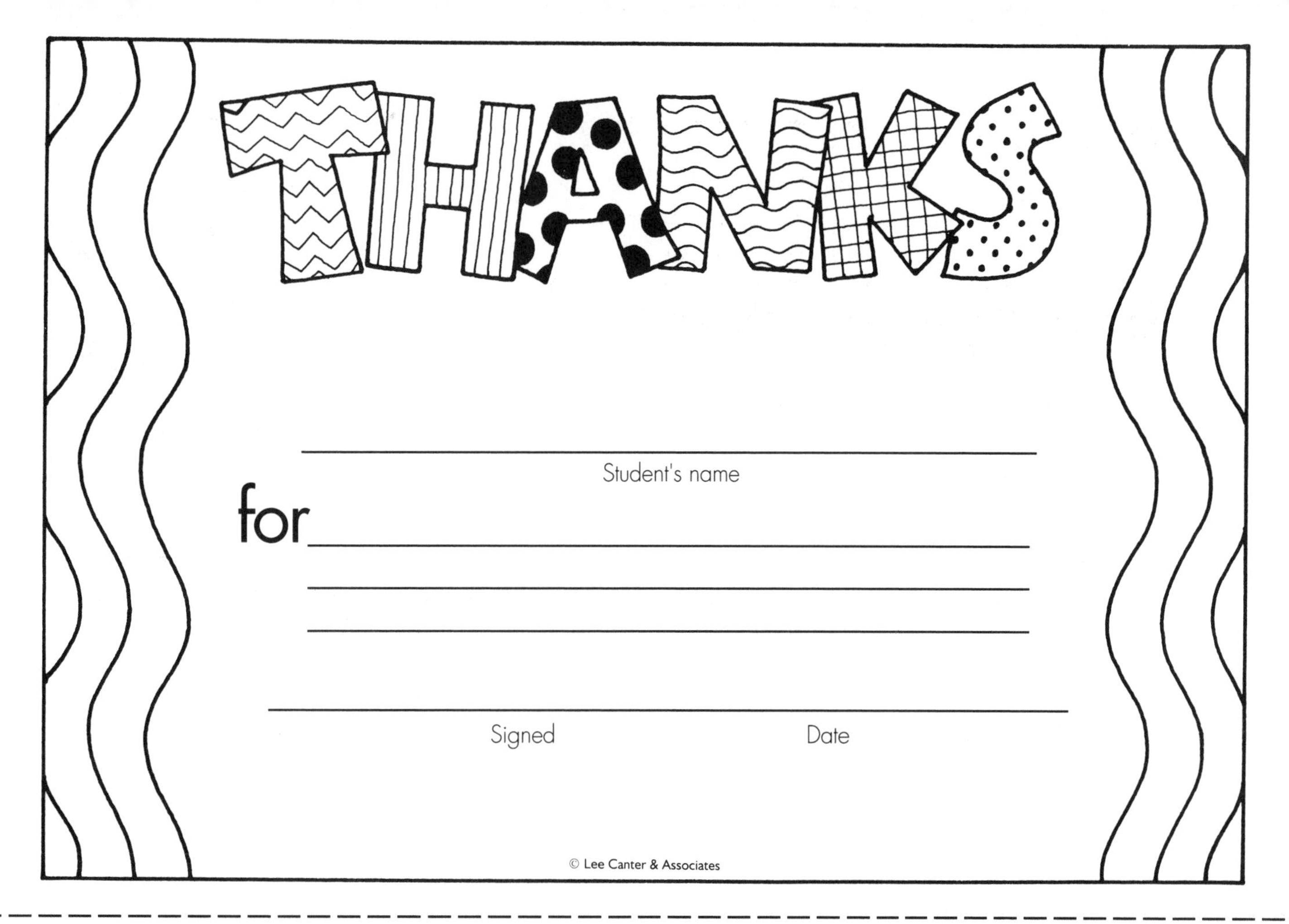
THANKS
Student's name
for
Signed
Date
© Lee Canter & Associates

To:
Student's name
Your behavior is something to celebrate.
Thanks!
Signed
Date
© Lee Canter & Associates

Special Privileges

Every student knows of something special that he or she enjoys doing at school. Some students love to be class monitor. Others appreciate free reading time. Still others find extra computer time a wonderful treat.

When you want to recognize positive student behavior, and motivate your students to continue that behavior, allow them to take part in activities that they particularly enjoy.

What do your students like to do? Here are some ideas to get you started. Add ideas of your own on the lines that follow.

- First in line
- Take care of the class pet
- Classroom monitor
- Correct papers
- Tutor younger children
- Help the teacher
- Free time
- Extra computer time
- Work on a favorite activity
- ____________________
- ____________________
- ____________________
- ____________________
- ____________________
- ____________________
- ____________________
- ____________________
- ____________________
- ____________________
- ____________________
- ____________________
- ____________________
- ____________________
- ____________________

It's Your Turn

Just ask 'em!

Not sure what special privileges will motivate your students? Give students the "My Favorite Activities" menu on the next page. We have started the menu with some activities that take place in most classrooms. Add your own to the list and ask students to check off three of their favorites. Older students can also write in suggestions of their own.

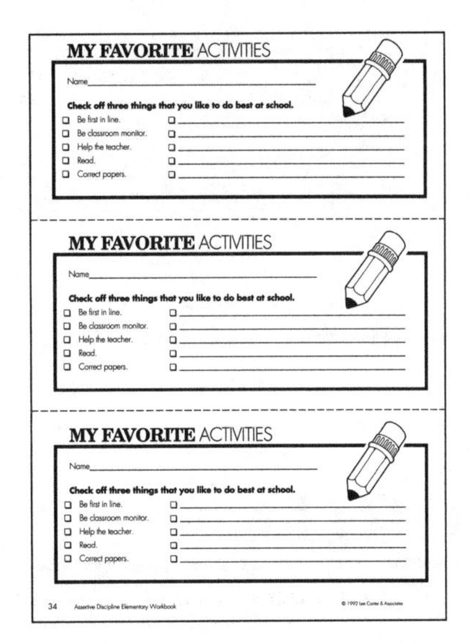

MY FAVORITE ACTIVITIES

Name

Check off three things that you like to do best at school.

- ☐ Be first in line.
- ☐ Be classroom monitor.
- ☐ Help the teacher.
- ☐ Read.
- ☐ Correct papers.

MY FAVORITE ACTIVITIES

Name

Check off three things that you like to do best at school.

- ☐ Be first in line.
- ☐ Be classroom monitor.
- ☐ Help the teacher.
- ☐ Read.
- ☐ Correct papers.

MY FAVORITE ACTIVITIES

Name

Check off three things that you like to do best at school.

- ☐ Be first in line.
- ☐ Be classroom monitor.
- ☐ Help the teacher.
- ☐ Read.
- ☐ Correct papers.

34 Assertive Discipline Elementary Workbook

© 1992 Lee Canter & Associates

Tell students that you want them to make these "menu" selections because throughout the year you will be awarding special privileges to students who behave responsibly at school. Tie this activity with a brief class discussion and you're sure to gather lots of motivating suggestions!

You Earned It!

When a student earns a special privilege for good behavior, fill out a "You Earned It!" coupon (page 35).

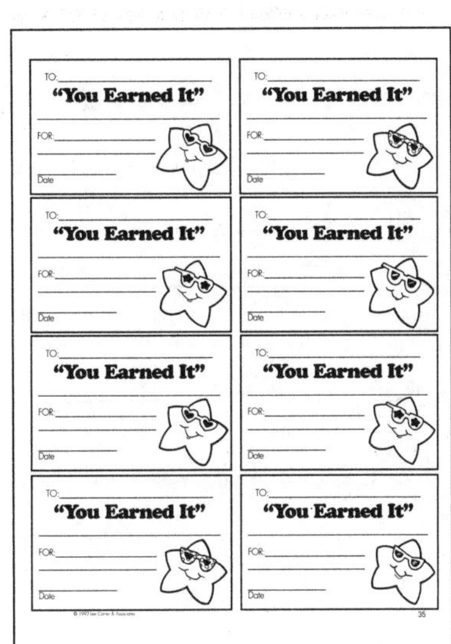

TO:
"You Earned It"
FOR:
Date

TO:
"You Earned It"
FOR:
Date

TO:
"You Earned It"
FOR:
Date

TO:
"You Earned It"
FOR:
Date

TO:
"You Earned It"
FOR:
Date

TO:
"You Earned It"
FOR:
Date

TO:
"You Earned It"
FOR:
Date

TO:
"You Earned It"
FOR:
Date

35

These open-ended coupons give students the good news and give you an easy way to present the positive recognition.

Sprinkle in some praise with your presentation and make the recognition even more meaningful.

> "You followed my directions so well, Andy, that you've earned the privilege of being first in line for lunch. Here's your reward coupon!"

MY FAVORITE ACTIVITIES

Name______________________________

Check off three things that you like to do best at school.

❑ Be first in line.	❑ ____________________
❑ Be classroom monitor.	❑ ____________________
❑ Help the teacher.	❑ ____________________
❑ Read.	❑ ____________________
❑ Correct papers.	❑ ____________________

MY FAVORITE ACTIVITIES

Name______________________________

Check off three things that you like to do best at school.

❑ Be first in line.	❑ ____________________
❑ Be classroom monitor.	❑ ____________________
❑ Help the teacher.	❑ ____________________
❑ Read.	❑ ____________________
❑ Correct papers.	❑ ____________________

MY FAVORITE ACTIVITIES

Name______________________________

Check off three things that you like to do best at school.

❑ Be first in line.	❑ ____________________
❑ Be classroom monitor.	❑ ____________________
❑ Help the teacher.	❑ ____________________
❑ Read.	❑ ____________________
❑ Correct papers.	❑ ____________________

TO:

"You Earned It"

FOR:

Date

TO:

"You Earned It"

FOR:

Date

TO:

"You Earned It"

FOR:

Date

TO:

"You Earned It"

FOR:

Date

TO:

"You Earned It"

FOR:

Date

TO:

"You Earned It"

FOR:

Date

TO:

"You Earned It"

FOR:

Date

TO:

"You Earned It"

FOR:

Date

Tangible Rewards

Most students are motivated by praise, positive notes and special privileges. You may, however, have one or two students who simply do not respond to these positive reinforcers. There are times when tangible rewards such as stickers or small trinkets are the only positives that will work—the only motivation a student will respond to. When needed, use tangible rewards, but use them with care.

Follow these guidelines:

- Be sure to give a tangible reward immediately after you have observed the desired behavior. You want the student to associate this behavior with the reward.
- Whenever you give a student a tangible reward, always pair it with your own praise such as,

  "Bobby, here's a sticker for sitting so quietly. I'm really proud of you."

  "Kelly, here's a pencil topper for taking your seat so quickly and quietly when you came into the classroom. By coming in so nicely we were able to listen to the story right away."

Tangible rewards are particularly effective on days when students tend to be overly excited, for example on Fridays and days before holidays.

It's Your Turn

We've looked at five ways you can positively reinforce students for following the rules of the classroom:

1 Praise

2 Positive notes and phone calls home

3 Special privileges

4 Behavior awards

5 Tangible awards

Now it's time to choose the positives you will use with individual students in your own classroom. Be sure to include positives that you are comfortable giving, and, most importantly, ones that you will be able to give frequently and consistently.

When you're finished planning, write the positives you have chosen on the poster on page 37. (Tuck the finished poster away with your supplies. You'll be using it when you introduce your classroom discipline plan to your students.)

POSITIVE RECOGNITION

____

____

____

____

____

POSITIVE
RECOGNITION
YEA
YES

Classwide Positive Recognition

Just as you recognize individual students for their appropriate behavior, you can also recognize your entire class for meeting expectations. A classwide positive recognition system makes it easy.

What is a classwide positive recognition system?

A classwide positive recognition system is a program in which all of your students, not just one student, work together toward a positive reward that will be given to the entire class.

The goal of a classwide recognition system is to motivate students to learn a new behavior or to work on improving a problem behavior. It shows students how important it is to work together in a cooperative manner to achieve a common goal.

Here's how to set up a classwide recognition program:

1. Pick a system that you are comfortable with and that is appropriate to the age of your students. (On pages 39-42 you will find directions and artwork for creating your own positive behavior bulletin board.)

2. Choose a reward that you are comfortable giving, but make sure that whatever the class earns, it is something they will want to work toward.

Here are some ideas for classwide rewards:

- Special movie or video
- Extra free time in class
- Special arts and crafts project
- Extra PE time
- Invite a special visitor to class.
- Popcorn party

3. Make sure students are able to earn the reward in a timely manner. Set a goal for how quickly you want the class to earn a reward. Then monitor the frequency with which you are awarding points to ensure that you and the students are on track.

Here are some suggested time frames for elementary students:

Grades K-1	1 day
Grades 2-3	2 days to 1 week
Grades 4-6	1 to 2 weeks

4. Once the class has earned points toward a classwide reward, do not take away points for misbehavior. Also, all students, regardless of negative consequences they may have earned individually, must participate in the classwide reward. If you impose a consequence and take away the classwide reward, you are providing two consequences for one misbehavior.

It's Your Turn

The following pages contain artwork and instructions for creating a positive behavior bulletin board.

We "GOPHER" Good Behavior BULLETIN BOARD

SUGGESTIONS FOR CONSTRUCTION

- Draw the underground gopher tunnel on brown paper. Divide the tunnel into spaces equal to the number of days students must demonstrate good behavior in order to achieve their goal and receive their classwide reward.

  For example: Grades K-3 — 5 spaces Grades 4-5 — 10 spaces

- Draw a 12" wide Finish Line hole where the tunnel emerges through the ground.
- Make grass from strips of green construction paper. Staple or pin to board as shown.
- Color and cut out the "We GOPHER Good Behavior!" sign (page 40). Place sign at beginning of the tunnel (see illustration).
- Color and cut out the large gopher (page 41).
- (Optional) Reproduce the "I Dig Good Behavior" gopher tags—one per student (page 42). Have each student color, cut out and write his or her name on the gopher tag. Pin all gopher tags around the border of the bulletin board.

SUGGESTIONS FOR USE

The object of this classwide recognition system is for the class to "tunnel" through the underground maze by behaving appropriately in class. Encourage all students to participate in reaching the final goal by jotting down points on the chalkboard during the day. Whenever you notice the entire class or an individual student behaving appropriately, praise the student(s) and chalk up a point! At the end of the day total the points. If the sum equals a predetermined number (such as 10, 20 or 30), move the large gopher one space ahead in the tunnel. The object of this activity is for the class to succeed every day and for the gopher to move through the tunnel in a week or two. Always be on the lookout for good behavior, especially with those difficult students who need positive recognition for their efforts. On the day the gopher emerges from the tunnel, reward the class with a special activity.

Room ______
We "gopher" good behavior

We "gopher"
good behavior

Creating Your Classroom Discipline Plan

Consequences* — not punishments

In spite of the care you take in choosing your rules, and in spite of your consistent attention to positive recognition, there will be times when students will choose not to follow the rules of your classroom. When this disruptive behavior occurs, you must be prepared to deal with it calmly and quickly.

Consequences are the third part of your classroom discipline plan.

Why are consequences important?

By carefully planning consequences, by knowing in advance what you will do when students misbehave, you won't be caught off guard or left wondering how to respond to a student's misbehavior. And that means that students will be treated fairly and you will feel less stress.

Follow these guidelines when choosing consequences for your classroom:

- **Consequences are a choice.**

It's important that consequences be presented to students as a choice. When a teacher gives students a choice, he or she places responsibility where it belongs, on the student.

For example:

Teacher: Sara, our classroom rule is no teasing. If you tease any student in this class, you will choose to sit by yourself and do your work. It's your choice.

Sara: Okay. *(Within a minute, Sara is teasing Ryan, the student who sits next to her.)*

Teacher: Sara, you're teasing Ryan. You have chosen to sit by yourself at the table in the back of the room.

Remember—**choice** is the key word. When you give students a choice, they learn that they can be in control of what happens to them. Keep in mind that consequences are not punishment. Consequences are actions students know will occur should they choose to break the rules of the classroom. Consequences must be seen as natural outcomes of inappropriate behavior.

- **Consequences do not have to be severe to be effective.**

Teachers often think that the more severe a consequence, the more impact it will have on a student. This is not true.

The key to effective consequences is that they are used consistently. It is the inevitability of the consequence, not the severity, that makes it effective. Minimal consequences, such as five minutes working away from the group, can be as effective as after-school detention when they are given consistently.

And the easier it is for you to give consequences, the more likely it will be that you will use them.

- **Consequences must be something that students do not like, but they must never be physically or psychologically harmful.**

* They are direct levels to not performing the needed behavior

How to Use Consequences:
Establishing a Discipline Hierarchy

The best way to use consequences with your students is to organize them into a discipline hierarchy as part of your classroom discipline plan.

A discipline hierarchy lists consequences in the order in which they will be imposed for disruptive behavior within a day.

- The hierarchy is progressive, starting with a warning.
- The consequences then become gradually more substantial for the second, third, fourth, and fifth time that a student chooses to disrupt.

Here's how the discipline hierarchy works:

First Time a Student Disrupts

Give a warning the first time a student disrupts or breaks a classroom rule.

This is an important first consequence because a warning gives the student an opportunity to choose more appropriate behavior before a more substantial consequence is received.

Second or Third Time a Student Disrupts

The second or third time a student disrupts in the same day, you need to provide a consequence.

These consequences should be easy to implement and not time consuming. Typical consequences for second or third infractions include time out and, for older students, writing in a behavior journal.

Fourth Time a Student Disrupts

Four disruptions during one day is completely unacceptable. You need to contact parents if a student disrupts a fourth time in a day.

For some students, involving parents will be the only way you will motivate them to behave appropriately. Students need to know that you will be consistent in the enforcement of this consequence.

Fifth Time a Student Disrupts

Sending a student to the principal should be the last consequence on your discipline hierarchy.

In preparation for implementing this consequence, you must have already met with the principal and discussed actions he or she will take when students are sent to the office (see pages 54-55).

Severe Clause

Sometimes you have to act quickly and decisively to stop a student's disruptive behavior. In cases of severe misbehavior, such as fighting, vandalism, defying a teacher or in some way stopping the entire class from functioning, a student would not receive a warning. He or she loses the right to proceed through the hierarchy of consequences. Severe misbehavior calls for an immediate consequence that will remove the student from the classroom.

Here are sample discipline hierarchies for elementary classrooms:

Sample Discipline Hierarchy for Grades K-3

First time a student breaks a rule:	~~Warning~~ Verbal Reminder
Second time:	5 minutes working away from the group
Third time:	10 minutes working away from the group
Fourth time:	Call parents
Fifth time:	Send to principal
Severe Clause:	Send to principal

Sample Discipline Hierarchy for Grades 4-5

First time a student breaks a rule:	~~Warning~~ Verbal Reminder
Second time:	10 minutes working away from the group
Third time:	15 minutes working away from the group plus write in behavior journal
Fourth time:	Call parents
Fifth time:	Send to principal
Severe Clause:	Send to principal

Keeping Track of Consequences

For your discipline hierarchy to be simple to use and easy to integrate into your teaching routine, you will need a system to keep track of student misbehavior and consequences accrued. You'll need to know at a glance the names of students who have received consequences, and where they are on the hierarchy.

Keeping track doesn't have to be time consuming and, most important, it doesn't have to interrupt your teaching.

On the following pages we will demonstrate two methods of keeping track of consequences: the Behavior Tracking Sheet and a Color-Coded Card system.

Using a Behavior Tracking Sheet

Here's how a Behavior Tracking Sheet works:

Make copies of the Behavior Tracking Sheet on page 47. Keep a sheet attached to a clipboard, and close by throughout the day.

Follow these guidelines:

First time a student breaks a rule
Write down his or her name on the sheet and say, for example, "Linda, the rule is 'Keep your hands to yourself.' This is a warning."

- Circle the "Warning" designation on the tracking sheet.

Second time a student breaks a rule
Speak quietly and calmly to the student saying, for example, "Linda, this is the second time you have misbehaved. You have chosen to sit by yourself in the back of the room."

- Circle the "2" on the tracking sheet, indicating that this is the second infraction of the day. The student goes to the time-out area.

Third, fourth or fifth time a student breaks a rule.
If a student breaks a rule a third, fourth or fifth time during the day, you must continue speaking quietly and calmly to the student, and continue recording the infractions on the tracking sheet. Make sure that the consequences are given according to your hierarchy. If your fourth consequence is "call parents," be sure that you make that phone call. The success of your discipline plan depends upon your consistency.

Note: Space is allotted on the tracking sheet for brief comments. For some students you may wish to jot down the rule broken. Then, if you notice a pattern of behavior developing, you will have documentation to help you solve that problem.

BEHAVIOR TRACKING SHEET WEEK OF ______

Name	MONDAY	TUESDAY	WEDNESDAY	THURSDAY	FRIDAY
Linda S.	(Warning) (2) 3 4 5	Warning 2 3 4 5	Warning 2 3 4 5	Warning 2 3 4 5	Warning 2 3 4 5
	Warning 2 3 4 5	Warning 2 3 4 5	Warning 2 3 4 5	Warning 2 3 4 5	Warning 2 3 4 5
	Warning 2 3 4 5	Warning 2 3 4 5	Warning 2 3 4 5	Warning 2 3 4 5	Warning 2 3 4 5
	Warning 2 3 4 5	Warning 2 3 4 5	Warning 2 3 4 5	Warning 2 3 4 5	Warning 2 3 4 5
	Warning 2 3 4 5	Warning 2 3 4 5	Warning 2 3 4 5	Warning 2 3 4 5	Warning 2 3 4 5
	Warning 2 3 4 5	Warning 2 3 4 5	Warning 2 3 4 5	Warning 2 3 4 5	Warning 2 3 4 5
	Warning 2 3 4 5	Warning 2 3 4 5	Warning 2 3 4 5	Warning 2 3 4 5	Warning 2 3 4 5
	Warning 2 3 4 5	Warning 2 3 4 5	Warning 2 3 4 5	Warning 2 3 4 5	Warning 2 3 4 5
	Warning 2 3 4 5	Warning 2 3 4 5	Warning 2 3 4 5	Warning 2 3 4 5	Warning 2 3 4 5
	Warning 2 3 4 5	Warning 2 3 4 5	Warning 2 3 4 5	Warning 2 3 4 5	Warning 2 3 4 5
	Warning 2 3 4 5	Warning 2 3 4 5	Warning 2 3 4 5	Warning 2 3 4 5	Warning 2 3 4 5
	Warning 2 3 4 5	Warning 2 3 4 5	Warning 2 3 4 5	Warning 2 3 4 5	Warning 2 3 4 5
	Warning 2 3 4 5	Warning 2 3 4 5	Warning 2 3 4 5	Warning 2 3 4 5	Warning 2 3 4 5
	Warning 2 3 4 5	Warning 2 3 4 5	Warning 2 3 4 5	Warning 2 3 4 5	Warning 2 3 4 5
	Warning 2 3 4 5	Warning 2 3 4 5	Warning 2 3 4 5	Warning 2 3 4 5	Warning 2 3 4 5
	Warning 2 3 4 5	Warning 2 3 4 5	Warning 2 3 4 5	Warning 2 3 4 5	Warning 2 3 4 5

To the teacher: When a student receives a warning, write the student's name on this tracking sheet. If a student breaks additional rules during that school day, circle each consequence on the appropriate box. For example, if a student receives a warning and chooses not to follow the rules again during the day, you would record (Warning) (2) (3) 4 5.

BEHAVIOR TRACKING SHEET

WEEK OF ______________________

Name	MONDAY	TUESDAY	WEDNESDAY	THURSDAY	FRIDAY
	Warning 2 3 4 5	Warning 2 3 4 5	Warning 2 3 4 5	Warning 2 3 4 5	Warning 2 3 4 5
	Warning 2 3 4 5	Warning 2 3 4 5	Warning 2 3 4 5	Warning 2 3 4 5	Warning 2 3 4 5
	Warning 2 3 4 5	Warning 2 3 4 5	Warning 2 3 4 5	Warning 2 3 4 5	Warning 2 3 4 5
	Warning 2 3 4 5	Warning 2 3 4 5	Warning 2 3 4 5	Warning 2 3 4 5	Warning 2 3 4 5
	Warning 2 3 4 5	Warning 2 3 4 5	Warning 2 3 4 5	Warning 2 3 4 5	Warning 2 3 4 5
	Warning 2 3 4 5	Warning 2 3 4 5	Warning 2 3 4 5	Warning 2 3 4 5	Warning 2 3 4 5
	Warning 2 3 4 5	Warning 2 3 4 5	Warning 2 3 4 5	Warning 2 3 4 5	Warning 2 3 4 5
	Warning 2 3 4 5	Warning 2 3 4 5	Warning 2 3 4 5	Warning 2 3 4 5	Warning 2 3 4 5
	Warning 2 3 4 5	Warning 2 3 4 5	Warning 2 3 4 5	Warning 2 3 4 5	Warning 2 3 4 5
	Warning 2 3 4 5	Warning 2 3 4 5	Warning 2 3 4 5	Warning 2 3 4 5	Warning 2 3 4 5
	Warning 2 3 4 5	Warning 2 3 4 5	Warning 2 3 4 5	Warning 2 3 4 5	Warning 2 3 4 5
	Warning 2 3 4 5	Warning 2 3 4 5	Warning 2 3 4 5	Warning 2 3 4 5	Warning 2 3 4 5
	Warning 2 3 4 5	Warning 2 3 4 5	Warning 2 3 4 5	Warning 2 3 4 5	Warning 2 3 4 5
	Warning 2 3 4 5	Warning 2 3 4 5	Warning 2 3 4 5	Warning 2 3 4 5	Warning 2 3 4 5
	Warning 2 3 4 5	Warning 2 3 4 5	Warning 2 3 4 5	Warning 2 3 4 5	Warning 2 3 4 5
	Warning 2 3 4 5	Warning 2 3 4 5	Warning 2 3 4 5	Warning 2 3 4 5	Warning 2 3 4 5

To the teacher: When a student receives a warning, write the student's name on this tracking sheet. If a student breaks additional rules during that school day, circle each consequence on the appropriate box. For example, if a student receives a warning and chooses not to follow the rules again during the day, you would record (Warning) (2) (3) 4 5.

Using the Color-Coded Card System for Tracking Behavior

This system is an easy way to monitor the behavior signals in your classroom—and it's simple to make. You will need a large sheet of poster board, a library pocket for each student and the reproducible "signals" on page 49.

Preparation:

1 Paste the library pockets onto the poster board (see illustration), writing the name of a student on the front of each library pocket.

2 Reproduce enough behavior "signal" sets so that each student can have a school zone signal, a green light signal, a yellow light signal and a red light signal.

3 Have each student cut out and color his or her signals and place them in the library pocket in this order: (front to back)—school zone, green light, yellow light and red light. Make sure that each student's name is on the back of each of his or her cards.

Directions for Use:

At the beginning of the school day, each student's pocket is arranged in order so that the school zone card is in front. This signifies that every student has started the day with a clean slate! If a student breaks a classroom rule and receives a warning, he or she removes the school zone card from the front of the pocket and places it behind all the other cards.

After the first consequence, the green card is showing.

For example:

> "Monica, the rule in our classroom is no running. That's a warning."
>
> *Monica quietly gets up, removes the school zone card from the front of her pocket, and places it behind all the other cards.*

If a student receives a second consequence in a day, the green card is removed, placed behind the other cards, and the yellow signal is in the front of the pocket. If a student should receive a third consequence within a day, the red signal shows in the pocket.

The red indicates the student is at the fourth consquence. At this point the parents or principal should be involved.

At the end of the school day all cards are put back in order for the beginning of the next day. The number of consequences received by any individual student may be recorded on a separate documentation sheet.

SCHOOL
ZONE
Green
Yellow
Red

Suggested Consequences

Here are consequences that have proven effective with elementary-age students:

Time Out—Removing a Student from the Group

Removing a disruptive student from the group is not a new concept, but it is a very effective consequence for elementary-age students. Designate a chair or table as the "time-out" area. Depending upon the age of the student, a trip to the time-out area could last from five to ten minutes.

> Note: It's very important that students not be isolated from the rest of the class for long lengths of time. Keep your time within these limits.

While separated from the rest of the class, the student continues to do his or her classwork.

Written Assignment in Behavior Journal

You want more from consequences than a student feeling contrite. You also want the student to learn from the experience. That's critical if a student is to learn to choose responsible behavior. You want him to think about his behavior, and how he can choose to behave differently in the future.

The following consequence is appropriate for upper-elementary students:

When a student breaks a classroom rule, have him write a "Behavior Journal" account of his misbehavior during recess, after class or at home. This written account should include the following points:

1. The rule that was broken.

   The rule I broke was no hitting.

2. Why the student chose to break the rule or not follow the direction.

   I hit Michael at recess because he was teasing me. He kept saying that my jacket was ugly.

3. What alternative action the student could have taken that would have been more appropriate.

   Instead of hitting Michael I could have ignored him. I could have walked away and played with someone else.

The student signs and dates the Behavior Journal sheet. The sheet should then be added to the student's documentation records. (It can also be sent home to parents as documentation of the student's misbehavior.)

Writing in a behavior journal helps students accept responsibility for their behavior. It also helps them think about choosing alternative behaviors in the future.

> Note: You may wish to use the Behavior Journal with younger students, too. Have students dictate their entries to you or to an aide. Then use this time as an opportunity to discuss the student's behavior, and how he or she can make better choices in the future.

It's Your Turn

On page 51 you will find a reproducible Behavior Journal sheet. Make copies of this sheet and use it as part of your discipline hierarchy.

Write the consequences you choose on the poster on page 52.

BEHAVIOR JOURNAL

Student's name ______________________________ Date____________

This is the rule I broke: ______________________________

____

I chose to break this rule because: ______________________________

____

____

____

____

____

____

____

____

____

This is what I could have done instead: ______________________________

____

____

____

____

____

Student Signature Date

CONSEQUENCES

SECTION TWO

Launching Your Classroom Discipline Plan

Your discipline plan is written. You've chosen the rules for your classroom, the positive recognition you will give when students follow the rules, and the consequences students will receive when they choose to break the rules.

Ready to put it all into action?

Not quite.

The success of your classroom discipline plan depends on more than your planning and involvement alone. It also depends on the informed involvement of others who will be affected by it: your students, your students' parents and your administrator.

In this section of the *Assertive Discipline Elementary Workbook* we will look at techniques for introducing your discipline plan. Also included is a selection of reproducibles to help you plan and carry out an effective introduction.

Talk to Your Principal About Your Classroom Discipline Plan

Your principal is an integral part of your behavior management program. No matter how well prepared you are, no matter how consistently and positively you use your discipline plan, you may still have one or two students that you will not be able to influence on your own. You are going to need the cooperation and assistance of your principal. The best way to ensure that cooperation is to involve him or her from the very beginning.

Before you put your classroom discipline plan into effect, you must meet with your principal to discuss his or her role in your discipline plan.

Involving your principal is important for two reasons.

First, if you send a student to the office, according to your discipline hierarchy, your principal will want to know what steps you have already taken.

Second, so that you can follow up with a student, you will want to know exactly what action the principal will take when a student is sent to him or her.

Make an appointment with your principal before school begins. Follow these guidelines for presenting your plan:

Explain your rationale for using a classroom discipline plan.

Begin by explaining why you are using a classroom discipline plan. Let your principal know that you are committed to having a classroom that is safe and orderly—a positive learning environment for your students, and a positive teaching environment for yourself. Explain that this is the reason you have established a classroom discipline plan with rules for behavior, positive recognition for students who choose to follow the rules and consequences for students who choose to break the rules.

Emphasize that you will attempt to handle behavior problems on your own before you ever ask for the principal's help.

Your principal needs to know that before you send a student to the office, you first will have taken steps to deal with the student on your own.

Ask the principal for input.

Have your principal read your plan. Ask for his input to make sure that he is comfortable with all aspects of the plan. If he is not comfortable, ask for assistance in modifying the plan.

Discuss what the principal will do when a student is sent from your class to the office.

You need to know exactly what will happen when you send a student to the principal.

Many principals follow a hierarchy of consequences, such as:

First time sent to office:
Counsel with the student and suggest other ways the student could have handled the situation.

Second time sent to office:
Hold a parent conference to discuss the problem. Ask parents to support the school's efforts by taking away privileges at home.

Third time sent to office:
In-school suspension. The student does schoolwork outside of the regular classroom and in a closely supervised environment.

Severe:
Counsel with the student and have a parent conference.

It is important that your principal lets you know what type of disciplinary action will be taken so you can follow up appropriately with parents and student. This can be accomplished by sending a note home or having a short meeting after school.

Discuss what will happen if the administrator is out of the building.

There may be times when you need to remove a disruptive student from your classroom and the principal is not in the building. Ask your principal what you should do in this circumstance.

Here are two alternatives:

- Send student to the school counselor.
- Send student to "time out" in another classroom.

With prior consent of another teacher, a disrupting student is sent to a higher grade classroom. When the student reaches the other classroom, she sits in a prearranged area away from the rest of the class. The student does not participate in the class activities and either sits quietly or does her own academic work.

Your administrator is an important part of your behavior management team. As such, he or she needs to be informed in advance of the involvement and support you expect. By introducing your discipline plan, you will assure your principal that you are prepared to deal with student misbehavior on your own before asking for adminstrative assistance. And by mututally establishing what action your principal will take, you will help ensure that discipline problems will be handled in a fair and consistent manner by both of you.

Teach Your Classroom Discipline Plan to Your Students

A list of rules posted on your classroom wall is not enough to motivate students to always follow those rules. You must actively involve your students in the plan.

Teaching your classroom discipline plan to your students is as important as any lesson you will teach during the year. This lesson should take place the first day of school.

The lesson should cover the following points:

1. Explain why you need rules.
2. Teach the rules.
3. Check for understanding.
4. Explain how you will reinforce students who follow the rules.
5. Explain why you have consequences.
6. Teach the consequences.
7. Check for understanding.

Here are some suggestions for teaching your lesson.

1. Explain why you need rules.
First, make sure that all students understand what rules are, and why they are needed. Talk about rules that students are already familiar with. Ask students to share comments about rules they have at home, or have had in other classrooms.

> "How many of you have rules at home?"
>
> "What are some of the rules?"
>
> "Why do you think your parents want you to follow rules at home?"
>
> "Why do you think we need rules at school?"
>
> "What might happen in a classroom without rules? Would this be good for all students? Would it be harder for us to learn?"

2. Explain your classroom rules.
Now you must clearly explain each of your classroom rules. Talk about why each rule is important, and why you have chosen it. For example, the rule "Walk, don't run in the classroom" is important for safety reasons, and for moving from one activity to another calmly and quickly. If appropriate, roleplay rules to aid understanding.

3. Check for understanding.
Now take the time to make sure that all students understand the rules you've taught. Have students repeat the rules in their own words. Then ask if there are any questions about the rules. Above all, make sure that students understand that these rules are in effect at all times—during all activities.

> "Sara, is there ever a time when it's OK to run in the classroom?"
>
> "Enrique, is it ever all right to hit another student?"
>
> "Calvin, when I give a direction, what should you do?"

4. Explain how you will reinforce students who follow the rules.
Positive reinforcement is going to be the most important part of your classroom discipline plan. Tell your students that you know they can all be successful at following the rules of the classroom, and that it will be your pleasure to recognize and reward those students who follow the rules. Pique student enthusiasm and motivation by detailing the positive reinforcement you will use.

> "See these good behavior bookmarks? I'll be giving these bookmarks to students who follow the rules. . . ."

5. Explain why you have consequences.
Students need to understand that they are responsible for the behavioral choices they make.

"Some of you may be wondering what will happen if you do not follow our rules. That's a fair question. After all, none of us is perfect. We all have trouble at times following rules. Let's talk about this.

"Who can tell me what might happen at home if you break an important rule? Do your parents ever say, 'No TV tonight' or 'You can't play after school?' Why do your parents do this? (*Share responses.*) Your parents do this to help you learn to behave in a safer way.

"At school I want to help you learn to behave in a safe way also. When you choose to break a classroom rule, you need to learn that something will happen. Something you probably won't like very much."

6. Explain the consequences.
Tell students exactly what will happen if they choose to misbehave once in a day, twice in a day, three times in a day, four times in a day and five times in a day. Explain how you will keep track of consequences.

"See this clipboard? (*Hold up.*) I'm going to keep it near me during the day. The first time you break a rule and disrupt the class, I will write your name on the clipboard. I'll also remind you of what the rules are. For example, if you are running in the classroom, all I will say to you is, 'John, the rule is no running in the classroom. That is a warning.' If you are teasing your neighbor, I'll say 'Sarah, the rule is no teasing. That's a warning.'

"That's all that I'll do.

"This warning gives you a chance to choose better behavior. And I know that you *will* choose better behavior.

"But if you do break this rule again, or any other rule during the day, I'll circle the 2 on the chart. This means that you've broken a rule two times. And this means that you have chosen to sit for five minutes in the time-out area. This will give you time to calm down and think about your behavior.

"The second time you break a rule in this class you will go to time out."

Go through the rest of your disciplinary hierarchy in this manner, explaining each consequence. Afterwards, take the time to emphasize your belief that the students can behave—and can act responsibly.

"I know that all of you can follow our classroom rules. I know that all of you can make good decisions about how to behave. I hope that none of you choose to go to time out, have me call your parents, or go to the principal."

7. Check for understanding.
It's important that all students understand the consequences you will use in your classroom. Ask students if they have any questions.

Keep this in mind: The manner in which you present your discipline plan to your students will set the tone for your classroom for the entire year. Be positive! Communicate your high expectations. Emphasize to your students that you believe they will all choose to follow the rules and enjoy the rewards of their good behavior. However, students must also understand that if they choose to break a rule, a consequence will follow.

Refer to pages 97-110 of the revised Assertive Discipline text for additional sample scripts for teaching this lesson.

It's Your Turn

Teaching your classroom discipline plan is an important lesson, one that will impact your classroom environment for the rest of the year. Take the time to carefully plan the lesson. Use the Lesson-Planning Worksheet on the following pages as you organize your lesson.

TEACHING YOUR CLASSROOM DISCIPLINE PLAN

LESSON PLANNING WORKSHEET

Use this worksheet to create your classroom discipline plan.

1. Explain why you need rules.

2. Explain the rules.

3. Check for understanding.

4. Explain how you will reinforce students who choose to follow the rules.

5. Explain why you have consequences.

6. Explain the consequences.

7. Check for understanding.

After you've taught the lesson. . .

Don't wait even one day to start reinforcing students for following your classroom rules. As soon as the lesson has been taught, look for opportunities to recognize students for good behavior and immediately begin reinforcing students who follow the rules.

Let students know that you notice and appreciate the good efforts they're making. Through your actions let them know that you mean what you said about positive reinforcement.

> "Jessica, good job following my directions today."
>
> "Richard, thank you for walking in the classroom."

It's Your Turn

These ideas will help you reinforce students' appropriate behavior at the start of the year.

Teacher's "Good Behavior" Badges

Encourage students' good behavior by wearing your own message of encouragement. These badges for teachers (page 62) will serve as constant reminders to students of your behavioral expectations and bring smiles to their faces as well. Use these badges in conjunction with the corresponding Desktop Behavior Charts (see below).

Desktop Behavior Charts

The Desktop Behavior Charts on page 63 will help you recognize and reinforce students who follow the rules. When you spot a student exhibiting good classroom behavior, stamp (or add a sticker to) his or her chart. These charts should be taped to each student's desk or kept in a special folder. When the chart, or a designated portion thereof, is filled in, the student receives a reward. When completely filled, the chart is taken home to show parents.

> "Good job following directions, Carol. That's another stamp on your chart!"

Beginning-of-the-Year Awards
Good habits start early in the year! The awards on pages 64-65 are specially designed to recognize students who follow the rules at the start of the school year.

Post rules reminders.
On pages 66-68 you will find eye-catching posters of general rules that are commonly found in elementary classrooms. If these rules are part of your plan, have students color the posters and display them in the room. Depending on the age of your students, you may also pass them out for students to color and take home.

An open-ended bordered poster is also included to use for other rules of your own, as well as a "School Is Cool When You Follow the Rules" poster that's applicable to any classroom.

Post your plan.
Display the Rules, Positive Recognition and Consequences posters (pages 11-12, 37 and 52) in your classroom as an ever-present reminder of your classroom discipline plan. (This is important information for classroom visitors, new students, and substitutes, too.) Depending on their age, you may wish to give your students copies of these posters to keep.

And as the year proceeds. . .
Review your classroom rules frequently at the start of the year. Review as needed as the year progresses. It's especially important to review classroom rules after vacations and on days when students are excited about special events (the day before a holiday, first day of snow, field-trip day, Halloween, etc.).

I'M STUCK ON
GOOD
BEHAVIOR
GOOD BEHAVIOR
MAKES ME SMILE
I
GOOD
BEHAVIOR

______________is stuck on good behavior!

___________is happy to follow the rules!

__________________________loves to behave!

To: ____________________
Student's name
Thanks for "pitching in" and getting this year off to a great start.
Signed
Date
© Lee Canter & Associates

To: ____________________,
Student's name
You're off to a "sunsational" start!
Thank you,
Signed
Date
© Lee Canter & Associates

Student's name

is off to a "doggone" good start!

Thanks,

Signed Date

Who has "blasted off" to a great start?

has!

Student's name

Thank you,

Signed Date

Follow directions.

Keep hands, feet and objects to yourself.

Do not leave the room without permission.

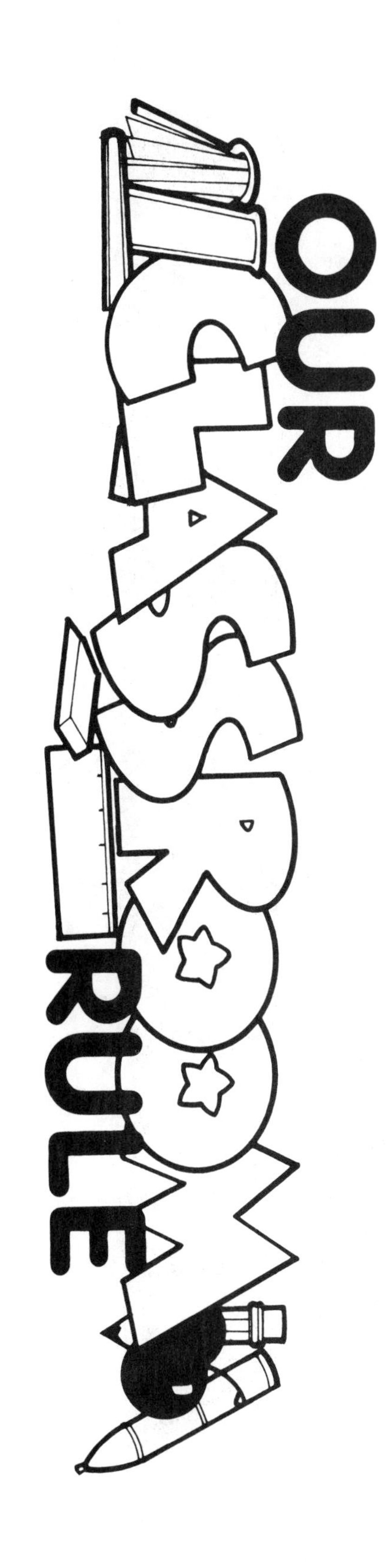
OUR
CLASSROOM
RULES

School is cool when you follow the rules.

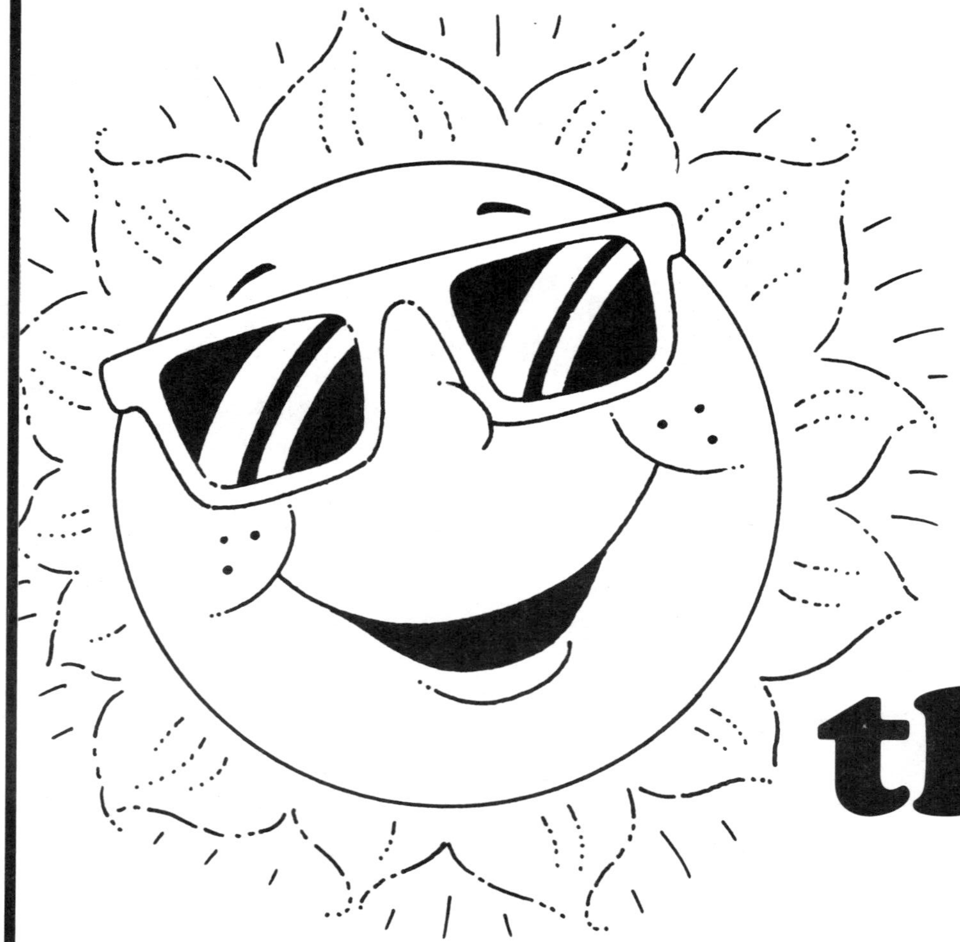

More Great Ideas!

Here are some ideas that will help you teach and reinforce your classroom discipline plan.

Grades K-1: Reading about Rules
Print one classroom rule on the lower part of a sheet of paper. Duplicate and pass out to students. Read the rule together. Talk once more about what the rule means. Ask students to draw a picture to go with the rule. Do this for each of your classroom rules. When completed, staple the three, four or five sheets together. As the year proceeds, use this booklet to help review and reinforce the rules.

Grades 2-4: Create a Rules Poster
Have students copy the rules from the classroom discipline plan onto lined paper. Then pass out large sheets of construction paper. Have each student glue the list of rules to the construction paper poster and title it "Classroom Rules." In their own words, have students write why this plan will help them learn to choose more responsible behavior in class.

Have students sign their posters, and you sign them, too. Students can take their posters home as reminders to parents, and themselves, of the classroom rules.

Grades 5-6: Create a Classroom Discipline Folder
Have students copy the classroom discipline plan as it is posted. Each student then places this copy in a Classroom Behavior folder. (The folder may also be used to keep copies of specific directions as explained on pages 78-88.) In a day or two, give a quick quiz on your classroom discipline plan. Tell students to use their copies of the plan to study.

Sample questions:

- Write down the four rules of our classroom.
- How many times a day do you receive a warning when you break a classroom rule?
- What happens the second time you break a rule?

Send Home a Copy of Your Discipline Plan to Parents

If parents are to become partners in their children's education, they must be well-informed about your classroom discipline plan. After all, contacting parents is part of your discipline hierarchy. You want them to be involved when you need them. Parents, therefore, need to be informed about why you have a plan and your rationale for rules, positive reinforcement and consequences.

Give each student a copy of your discipline plan to take home to parents. In an accompanying letter, explain why a classroom discipline plan is important, and ask parents to go over the plan with their child, sign the plan, and send it back to you.

Tell your students:

"Before you go home today, each of you will receive a copy of this letter to your parents. This letter explains our classroom discipline plan. I want all of you to talk with your parents about the plan. After you have talked about the plan, I want you and your parents to sign the bottom of the sheet. Please bring the tear-off portion back to me. I want all of your parents to know what I expect of you. And I want them to know that we will be working together to make sure this is a successful, happy year for all of you."

Your letter to parents should include the following:

- Your reason for having a classroom discipline plan.
- A list of the rules, positive reinforcement and negative consequences that are included in your plan.
- A message asking parents to support your discipline plan.
- An invitation for parents to call you with any concerns they might wish to discuss.
- A parent signature and comment sheet.

It's Your Turn

Copy your discipline plan on the Classroom Discipline Plan letterhead on page 74. Use the sample letter on page 73 as a guide for writing your own letter.

Substitute Support

You can't always be there every day. But you can make sure that your classroom continues to run smoothly—no matter who is in charge. To ensure consistent discipline in your classroom, even when you are not present, prepare a discipline plan for substitutes. Fill in your discipline plan on the Substitute Sheet on page 75. Make sure that a copy is left in the office. Put another copy in your lesson plan book or tape it to the top of your desk.

Also: The rules of your classroom must be in effect at all times. Therefore, it is important that any paraprofessionals or volunteers who work in your room understand the discipline plan and the role they are to play in its implementation. Take time to explain the plan to your support staff. Make it very clear how they are to deal with both positive and negative behavior.

Dear Parent:

I am delighted that your child ______________________________ is in my class this year.

I have developed a classroom discipline plan which affords every student guidance in making good decisions about his or her behavior and thus an opportunity to learn in a positive, nurturing classroom environment. Your child deserves the most positive educational climate possible for his or her growth, and I know that together we will make a difference in this process. The plan below outlines our classroom rules, positive rewards and consequences for appropriate and inappropriate behavior.

Rules:
1. Follow directions.
2. Keep hands, feet and objects to yourself.
3. No swearing or teasing.
4. Do not leave the classroom without permission.

To encourage students to follow our rules, I will recognize appropriate behavior with praise, and positive notes and phone calls home.

However, if a student chooses to break a rule, the following steps will be taken:

First time a student breaks a rule:	Warning
Second time:	5 minutes working away from the group
Third time:	10 minutes working away from the group
Fourth time:	Call parents
Fifth time:	Send to principal
Severe Disruption:	Send to principal

Please ask your child to review this classroom plan with you, and then sign and return the form below. Don't hesitate to contact me if you have any questions about this plan or any other matter.

____

Teacher's Signature Room Number Date

- -

I have read the classroom discipline plan and have discussed it with my child, ____________________

____

Parent/Guardian Signature Date

Comments____

____

____

CLASSROOM
plan

SUBSTITUTE'S PLAN

From the desk of: ______________________________

Dear Substitute:

The following are the guidelines for the discipline plan used in my classroom. Please follow them exactly, and leave me a list of students who break the rules and a list of students who behave properly.

Classroom Rules

1______________________________
2______________________________
3______________________________
4______________________________

Consequences

When a student breaks a rule:
1st time ______________________________
2nd time ______________________________
3rd time ______________________________
4th time ______________________________
5th time ______________________________

Severe Clause: If a student exhibits severe misbehavior such as fighting, open defiance or vulgar language, the following consequence is to be immediately imposed:

____

Students who behave will be rewarded when I return with:

____
____

In addition, please offer plenty of praise and positive recognition to students who follow the rules. They'll appreciate it!

Thank you for following my classroom discipline plan.

Sincerely,

S E C T I O N   T H R E E

Teaching Responsible Behavior

Developing your classroom discipline plan and teaching this plan to your students are the first steps you take to help them choose the responsible behavior that will enable them to succeed in school.

The next step is to teach your students how to make responsible behavioral choices in all situations at school.

In this section of the *Assertive Discipline Elementary Workbook* we will look at a variety of techniques that will help you motivate the majority of your students to behave appropriately.

Also included in this section is a wide selection of reproducibles that will help you implement these techniques.

Determining and Teaching Specific Directions

Your classroom discipline plan lists the general rules of your classroom. As you have seen, these rules are in effect at all times.

The most important of these classroom rules is, "Follow directions." This rule is included to ensure that students promptly follow *any* direction you might give during the day.

To comply with this rule, students must understand what each specific direction you give means. You can never assume that a roomful of young students will all follow a direction in the same way. And you can certainly never assume that a roomful of students will follow a direction according to *your* expectations.

- Do your students know how you expect them to line up?
- Do they know how you expect them to transition from one activity to another?
- Do they know how you expect them to work together in groups?

There are many ways to go about following any direction. If you want all your students to follow a direction in the same way, you must teach them. Right at the beginning of the year you need to take the time to teach your students exactly how you want them to behave in all classroom situations. You need to teach and reteach your expectations until every student knows how to line up, how to transition from one activity to another, and how to work in groups. Remember, the goal is for the student to succeed.

The more time you spend at the beginning of the year teaching your specific directions, the less time you'll spend *repeating* them as the year goes by.

Here's what to do:

First, identify the academic activities, routine procedures and special procedures for which specific directions are needed.

Next, determine the specific directions you want your students to follow for each activity and procedure you've identified.

Here are examples of academic activities:

- When you are giving a directed lesson in front of the class
- When students are doing independent seatwork
- When students are working in small groups doing cooperative learning tasks
- When the class is having a group discussion
- When students are taking a test
- When students are working at centers

Here are examples of routine procedures:

- When students enter the classroom
- When students leave the classroom
- When a student wants a drink of water
- When a student needs to use the restroom
- When a student needs to sharpen his or her pencil
- When students turn in homework
- When the teacher gives a signal to begin an activity
- When students transition from one activity to another
- When students are sitting in circle time
- When the teacher is taking attendance
- When the phone rings or a PA announcement is heard

Special Procedures

- When the fire drill bell rings
- When the class goes to a school assembly
- When the class goes on a field trip
- When guests come to the classroom
- When students are at the library

Note: Music teachers, art teachers, PE teachers and teachers who work in other special situations have to come up with a list of the activities and procedures that apply to their students.

For example:

- Putting music equipment away
- Putting sports equipment away
- Cleaning up after an art activity

The Difference Between Rules and Directions

- **Rules** are posted in your classroom, and are in effect at all times during the day.

- **Directions** are in effect for the duration of a specific activity. Directions may change based on the needs of the teacher and maturity level of the students.

It's Your Turn

Now think about a typical week in your own classroom. Start at the beginning of the school day on Monday and work your way through to the end of the day on Friday. Identify the academic activities, routine procedures and special procedures your students will be engaged in. Try not to leave anything out. List all of these on the following Specific Directions Worksheet.

SPECIFIC DIRECTIONS WORKSHEET

Use this worksheet to list all the academic activities, routine procedures and special procedures that occur during the school week.

Academic Activities

- ______________________
- ______________________
- ______________________
- ______________________
- ______________________
- ______________________
- ______________________
- ______________________
- ______________________
- ______________________
- ______________________
- ______________________

Routine Procedures

- ______________________
- ______________________
- ______________________
- ______________________
- ______________________
- ______________________
- ______________________
- ______________________
- ______________________
- ______________________
- ______________________
- ______________________

Special Procedures

- ______________________
- ______________________
- ______________________
- ______________________
- ______________________
- ______________________
- ______________________
- ______________________
- ______________________
- ______________________
- ______________________
- ______________________

Now, determine the specific directions you want your students to follow.

After you've listed all the activities for which you need specific directions, it's time to decide on those directions. It's not as complicated as it might sound. When determining the specific directions you want your students to follow, use these guidelines:

- **Keep it simple!**

Choose a limited number of specific directions for each classroom activity.

- **Choose directions that are observable.**

Your directions must be observable and easy for students to follow. Don't include vague directions such as "act good" or "behave appropriately."

- **Relate your directions to:**

1 How you want students to participate in the activity or procedure—*what you expect them to do.*

2 How you expect students to *behave* in order to be successful in the activity.

Here are some examples of specific directions for an elementary classroom:

Academic Activity: When the teacher is teaching a lesson in front of the class.

1 Clear your desks of everything but paper and pencil.

2 Eyes on me, or eyes on your paper. No talking while I'm talking.

(These directions let students know what they are expected to do.)

3 Raise your hand and wait to be called upon to ask or answer a question. Don't shout out answers.

(This direction lets students know how you expect them to behave.)

Academic Activity: When students are working independently.

1 Have all necessary books, paper, pencils and other materials on your desk.

2 Begin working on your assignment as soon as you receive it.

(These directions let students know what they are expected to do.)

3 No talking. Raise your hand to ask a question.

(This direction lets students know how you expect them to behave.)

Routine Procedure: When students enter the classroom.

1 Walk into the room.

2 Go directly to your seat and sit down.

(These directions let students know what they are expected to do.)

3 No talking after the bell rings.

(This direction lets students know how you expect them to behave.)

Special Procedure: Assemblies

1 Put books and materials away.

2 Without talking, walk at a normal pace to the door. Line up in a single file. No talking in line.

3 Line leader opens the door. Without talking, class walks to the cafeteria.

4 No talking during the assembly.

5 Return to class in a single line. No talking.

It's Your Turn

Write the specific directions for the classroom activities that apply to your own teaching situation. We've started the list with some activities that generally take place in all classrooms. Add to this list as needed.

Activity: When students arrive in the classroom in the morning.

1 ______________________________

2 ______________________________

3 ______________________________

Activity: When it is time for recess.

1 ______________________________

2 ______________________________

3 ______________________________

Activity: When students enter the classroom after recess.

1 ______________________________

2 ______________________________

3 ______________________________

Activity: When it's time to clean up.

1 ______________________________

2 ______________________________

3 ______________________________

Activity: When the class goes to the school library.

1 ______________________________

2 ______________________________

3 ______________________________

Now write directions for any other classroom activities you listed on page 80.

Activity: ______________________________

1 ______________________________

2 ______________________________

3 ______________________________

Activity: ______________________________

1 ______________________________

2 ______________________________

3 ______________________________

Activity: ______________________________

1 ______________________________

2 ______________________________

3 ______________________________

Activity: ______________________________

1 ______________________________

2 ______________________________

3 ______________________________

Activity: ______________________________

1 ______________________________

2 ______________________________

3 ______________________________

Activity: ______________________________

1 ______________________________

2 ______________________________

3 ______________________________

Activity: ______________________________

1 ______________________________

2 ______________________________

3 ______________________________

Activity: ____________________

1 ____________________

2 ____________________

3 ____________________

Activity: ____________________

1 ____________________

2 ____________________

3 ____________________

Activity: ____________________

1 ____________________

2 ____________________

3 ____________________

Activity: ____________________

1 ____________________

2 ____________________

3 ____________________

Activity: ____________________

1 ____________________

2 ____________________

3 ____________________

Activity: ____________________

1 ____________________

2 ____________________

3 ____________________

Activity: ____________________

1 ____________________

2 ____________________

3 ____________________

Activity: ____________________

1 ____________________

2 ____________________

3 ____________________

Activity: ____________________

1 ____________________

2 ____________________

3 ____________________

Activity: ____________________

1 ____________________

2 ____________________

3 ____________________

Activity: ____________________

1 ____________________

2 ____________________

3 ____________________

Activity: ____________________

1 ____________________

2 ____________________

3 ____________________

Activity: ____________________

1 ____________________

2 ____________________

3 ____________________

Activity: ____________________

1 ____________________

2 ____________________

3 ____________________

Teach your specific directions.

Once you've determined your specific directions, your goal in teaching them is not to simply pass along instructions, but to make this process a learning experience for students as well.

Teach students *why* your directions are important to everyone's well being. When students understand the reasons behind your directions, they'll be much more likely to follow them.

Why teach specific directions with such care?

Here are two good reasons:

- Teaching your specific directions ensures that behavior problems will be reduced during all academic activities, routine procedures and special procedures.
- Teaching specific directions increases a student's opportunity to succeed at those activities.

As with any successful lesson, preparation is vital to meeting your objectives. The lesson sequence that follows highlights points you'll want to include in your own specific directions lessons. Use this lesson as a guideline for developing a lesson for any specific direction. Keep in mind that your own lessons will differ, based on the age of your students and the directions you are teaching, but the focus of **explanation**, **teaching** and **checking for understanding** remains the same.

Grades K-3

With younger students you will want to spend plenty of time teaching and reinforcing each specific direction lesson. Give students the opportunity to role-play the directions, and give them ample opportunities to follow the directions after the lesson is given. Reteach and reinforce often. Use pictures or other visual clues to help reinforce the directions.

Grades 4-6

Students in grades 4-6 want to understand the reasons behind the directions they are expected to follow. Explain why they need to follow this direction and what the benefit will be to them and the other students.

Here's a sample lesson sequence for teaching specific directions:

1. Explain the rationale for the direction.

Students need to understand why your directions are important. Explain why they need to follow this direction and what the benefit will be to them and to other students.

> "Several times each day I will give you the direction to line up at the door. You'll hear this direction every day before recess, before lunch time, and before PE. So that we all can leave the classroom safely and quickly, it's important to follow directions when you line up."

2. Involve the students by asking questions.

Students will follow your directions more readily if you involve them in a discussion that rationally addresses your concerns.

> "Why do you think I want you to follow certain directions when you line up at the door? What could happen if we had no directions at all to follow? Do you think that we'd all do the same thing?"
>
> "Jenny, what would you do? Would you put your books away before you line up?"
>
> "Sam, would you stop on the way to take a drink of water?"
>
> "William, would you go get your jacket first?"
>
> "How many of you would rush to be first?"
>
> "Now, what could happen if some of you rushed to get a drink of water, some of you raced to the door, some of you went to get your jackets and some of you just talked at your desks?"
>
> "I think you can see why it's a good idea for all of us to be doing the same thing at the same time."

3. Explain the specific directions.
Now teach the students the directions they are to follow.

> "All right, these are the directions we are going to follow when it's time to line up at the door. When I say, 'Class, line up at the door,' this is what I expect you to do: First, I want you to put all of your books, pencils, paper and any other materials into your desk. Second, I want you to stand and quietly push your chair under your desk. And third, I want you to walk quietly, without talking, to the door and line up."

4. Check for understanding.
Check for understanding by asking students to restate the directions. Then reinforce the directions further by writing them on the board. (With K-1 students, you might choose to show a poster that pictorially illustrates the directions.)

> "All right, who can raise their hand and tell me what you will do first when I give the direction to line up at the door?"

Next, have students role-play the directions.

> "Let's practice what you've just learned. When I give the direction, I want you all to follow the directions you've just learned and line up at the door. Ready? Class, please line up at the door."

The teacher immediately begins to praise those students who are following the direction.

> "Mary has put her books away and is lining up. Kyle is walking quietly to the door. Jeff is putting his chair under his desk. Good work!"
>
> "Now, does anyone have any questions about how to line up at the door?"

After you've taught a specific directions lesson. . .

Immediately follow up any specific directions lesson with the activity or procedure that has just been taught. Be sure to reinforce students who follow the directions appropriately, and give reminders (or reteach if necessary) to those students who don't.

First Two Weeks
Review directions each time the class engages in the activity.

First Month
Review directions each Monday (as a reminder and refresher for the week to come).

Remainder of Year
Review directions as needed. It is especially important to review directions after a vacation, or on special days when students are excited (field trips, day before a vacation, Halloween).

Refer to pages 128-136 of the revised Assertive Discipline text for additional guidelines for teaching specific directions to your students.

It's Your Turn

Here are some ideas that will help you teach specific directions to your students.

Plan your lessons.

Use the Specific Directions Planning Sheet on the next two pages to plan the lessons you will teach. Run off plenty of copies and use them to write down questions you want to ask students during the lesson, points you want to make, and other reminders to yourself.

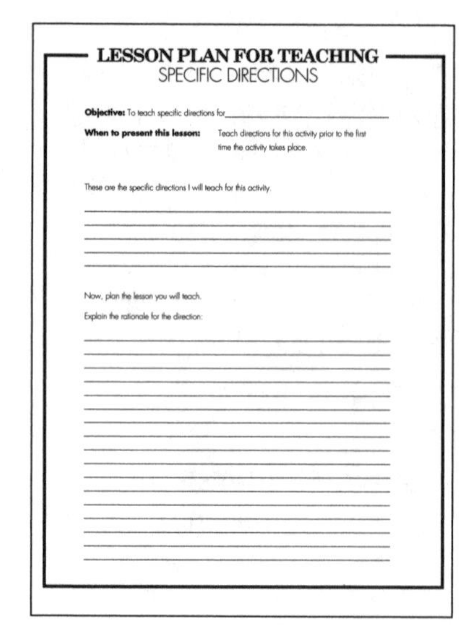

LESSON PLAN FOR TEACHING
SPECIFIC DIRECTIONS

Objective: To teach specific directions for________________

When to present this lesson: Teach directions for this activity prior to the first time the activity takes place.

These are the specific directions I will teach for this activity.

Now, plan the lesson you will teach.

Explain the rationale for the direction:

Post your directions.

Visual reminders can often help students remember directions. Use the open-ended poster on page 91 to create handy reminders of your directions.

Entering the Room

1. Walk into the room.
2. Go directly to your seat and sit down.
3. No talking after the bell rings.

Recognize students who follow directions.

The reproducible awards on pages 92-94 will help you recognize students who follow directions.

Create a Classroom Directions Binder

As new students enter your class throughout the year they too will need to learn your specific directions. This idea (for grades 2 and up) can help ease their transition and involve peers in the teaching process:

Use the open-ended "Directions for ________________" worksheet on page 91 to create direction sheets for different activities.

Organize these sheets into a looseleaf binder. Ask a student to decorate a cover sheet to create an inviting notebook that will be part of your classroom all year long. When a new student joins the class, assign him or her a buddy. It's the responsibility of the buddy to go through the binder with the new student and explain each of these directions.

LESSON PLAN FOR TEACHING
SPECIFIC DIRECTIONS

Objective: To teach specific directions for_______________________________

When to present this lesson: Teach directions for this activity prior to the first time the activity takes place.

These are the specific directions I will teach for this activity.

____

____

____

____

____

Now, plan the lesson you will teach.

Explain the rationale for the direction:

____

____

____

____

____

____

____

____

____

____

____

____

____

____

____

____

____

Involve the students by asking questions:

Explain the specific directions:

Check for understanding:

Notes on the lesson:

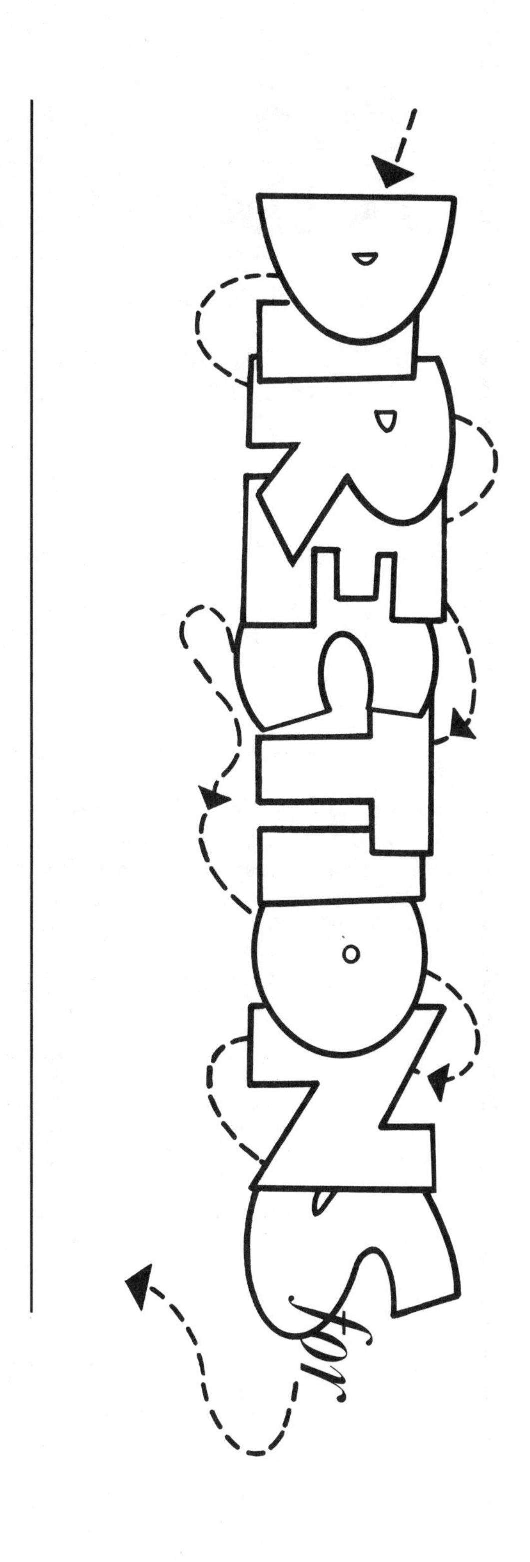
DIRECTIONS
for

Congratulations, ______________________!

You were "caught" following directions!

Good Job!

____
Signed   Date

To: ______________________

Thanks for following directions!

____
Signed   Date

To: ______________________________

I'd like to say a few words about the way you follow directions in class...

TERRIFIC!

SUPER!

GOOD JOB!

____
Signed Date

Take a bow,

____
Student's name

for following directions in our class —

You're helping us set the stage for a great year!

____
Signed Date

Student's name

was "caught" following directions.

Signed Date

Student's name

was "caught" following directions.

Signed Date

Way to go,

______________!

Student's name

You were "caught" following directions.

Signed

Student's name

was "caught" following directions.

Signed Date

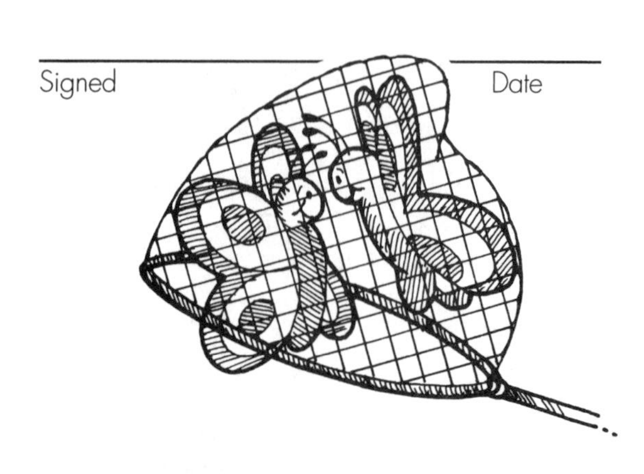

Teaching Responsible Behavior

Using Positive Recognition to Motivate Students to Behave

Once you've taught your students directions for all classroom activities, your goal is to help them be successful in following those directions.

Positive recognition is the most effective way to achieve this goal.

We will give you a variety of techniques that you can use to motivate students to choose appropriate behavior and then to *continue* that behavior.

These techniques are:

1 Positive Repetition

2 Consistent Praise

3 Scanning

4 Circulating the Classroom

On the following pages you will learn how to use each of these techniques throughout the day—while you teach, and while you are involved in any classroom activity.

Keep positive recognition techniques at your fingertips with Assertive Discipline Cue Cards.

What are Assertive Discipline Cue Cards?

Cue Cards are a quick and easy way to keep Assertive Discipline techniques close at hand and in your mind. All of the positive recognition techniques listed in this chapter, and other behavior management techniques included in upcoming chapters, have been organized into easy-to-use Assertive Discipline Cue Cards.

These reproducible Cue Cards give you portable, to-the-point references for successfully handling both appropriate and inappropriate classroom behavior.

Here are some guidelines for using the Cue Cards:

- **Read**
  Read each Cue Card. Think about how you can use each of these techniques in the day-to-day routine of your classroom.
- **Keep**
  Laminate the Cue Cards and then tuck them into the back of your lesson plan book for easy reference. From time to time review the techniques and make sure you are using them—effectively *and* consistently.
- **Share**
  Give a set of Cue Cards to your classroom aide or to parent volunteers. Encourage them to read the cards and use the techniques with students.

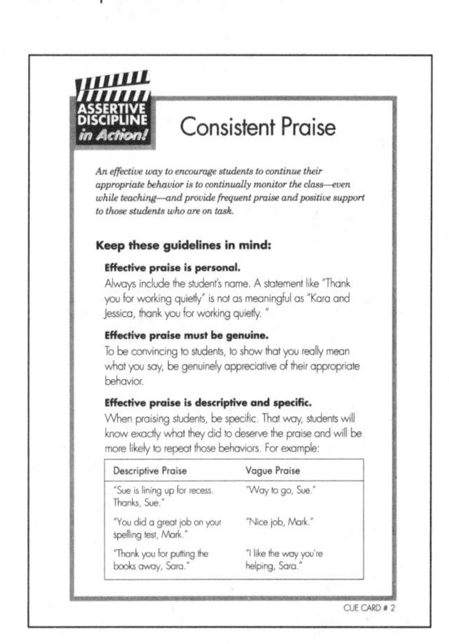

ASSERTIVE DISCIPLINE *in Action!*

Consistent Praise

An effective way to encourage students to continue their appropriate behavior is to continually monitor the class—even while teaching—and provide frequent praise and positive support to those students who are on task.

Keep these guidelines in mind:

Effective praise is personal.
Always include the student's name. A statement like "Thank you for working quietly" is not as meaningful as "Kara and Jessica, thank you for working quietly."

Effective praise must be genuine.
To be convincing to students, to show that you really mean what you say, be genuinely appreciative of their appropriate behavior.

Effective praise is descriptive and specific.
When praising students, be specific. That way, students will know exactly what they did to deserve the praise and will be more likely to repeat those behaviors. For example:

Descriptive Praise	Vague Praise
"Sue is lining up for recess. Thanks, Sue."	"Way to go, Sue."
"You did a great job on your spelling test, Mark."	"Nice job, Mark."
"Thank you for putting the books away, Sara."	"I like the way you're helping, Sara."

CUE CARD # 2

ASSERTIVE
DISCIPLINE
in Action!

Positive Repetition

This technique will help encourage students to follow the many directions you give each day. It's called positive repetition.

Here's how positive repetition works:

1 Give a direction.

2 Immediately look for at least two students who are following the direction.

3 Say the students' names and restate the direction as they are following it.

Examples:

Direction:
"Please take your places on the reading mat."
Positive Repetition:
"Jennifer and Danny are already on their places on the reading mat."

Direction:
"Line up quickly and quietly."
Positive Repetition:
"Debbie is in line. That was very fast! Seth is in his place, too."

CUE CARD # 1

Guidelines for Frequency of Positive Repetition

At the beginning of the year you will be placing a heavy emphasis on teaching students how to behave. The more you want to teach children how to behave, the more you need to use praise. Thus, at the beginning of the year you will use positive repetition much more frequently than you will once your students learn what you need them to do in each classroom situation. Remember, one of the goals of positive reinforcement is to start strong, then gradually decrease the frequency.

Weeks 1-2 — Use positive repetition every time you give a direction. Don't worry about overdoing it.

Weeks 2-4 — Use positive repetition every third time you give a direction.

After first month: Use positive repetition every fourth time you give a direction. Maintain this frequency level throughout the year.

Positive repetition is a positive advantage for you and your students!

You give hundreds of directions in a week. And each time you give a direction you have a ready-made opportunity to positively reinforce students. When you get into the habit of using this technique, you will be assured that you will make more positive than negative statements to students.

ASSERTIVE
DISCIPLINE
in Action!

Consistent Praise

An effective way to encourage students to continue their appropriate behavior is to continually monitor the class—even while teaching—and provide frequent praise and positive support to those students who are on task.

Keep these guidelines in mind:

Effective praise is personal.
Always include the student's name. A statement like "Thank you for working quietly" is not as meaningful as "Kara and Jessica, thank you for working quietly. "

Effective praise must be genuine.
To be convincing to students, to show that you really mean what you say, be genuinely appreciative of their appropriate behavior.

Effective praise is descriptive and specific.
When praising students, be specific. That way, students will know exactly what they did to deserve the praise and will be more likely to repeat those behaviors. For example:

Descriptive Praise	Vague Praise
"Sue is lining up for recess. Thanks, Sue."	"Way to go, Sue."
"You did a great job on your spelling test, Mark."	"Nice job, Mark."
"Thank you for putting the books away, Sara."	"I like the way you're helping, Sara."

CUE CARD # 2

ASSERTIVE
DISCIPLINE
in Action!

Scanning

The scanning technique for motivating students to stay on task is useful when you are working with a small group of students, or an individual student, and the rest of the class is working independently.

Here's how to use the scanning technique:

1 When you are working with a small group, look up every few minutes and scan the students who are working independently.

2 As you notice students who are working appropriately, take a moment to recognize their good behavior.

"Robert is working quietly on his social studies assignment. Thank you, Robert."

3 The student will appreciate the recognition and continue working independently. Other students will get the message that you are aware of what's going on in the room, and will be motivated to stay on task themselves.

CUE CARD # 3

ASSERTIVE
DISCIPLINE
in Action!

Circulating the Classroom

While students are working independently, circulate the room and give positive recognition. One-on-one, you can let a student know that you recognize his or her appropriate behavior. This positive recognition is given quietly—a special message from the teacher to the student.

> "Mike, you are doing a great job on your science questions. You're going to finish the entire assignment!"
>
> "Andrew, you've been very cooperative today. You are doing a great job getting along with everyone."

There is no need to ever phase out this technique. Each time you circulate the classroom you have an opportunity to show your students you care, and that you notice their good efforts.

CUE CARD # 4

Teaching Responsible Behavior
Redirecting Non-Disruptive Off-task Behavior

By giving your students consistent positive recognition, you can eliminate the majority of problems before they even begin.

Experience has perhaps shown you, however, that there still will be students who behave inappropriately. This behavior can take two forms: disruptive off-task behavior and non-disruptive off-task behavior.

Disruptive Off-task Behaviors
Shouting out in class

Throwing paper airplanes

Pushing or shoving

Running in the classroom

Non-disruptive Off-task Behaviors
Looking out the window

Reading instead of listening

Doodling instead of working

Daydreaming

We will take a closer look at disruptive off-task behavior, and how to deal with it, on pages 105-108. Now we will focus on how to respond to non-disruptive off-task behavior—behavior in which a student is not disrupting others, but he's not paying attention or following directions, either.

As any teacher knows, students often fall into non-disruptive off-task behavior. After all, it doesn't take much for a first grader to start doodling on his paper, or for a fifth grader to lose interest in class and begin to stare out the window.

The teacher's responsibility is to guide the student back into learning.

Here's what you *don't* want to do:
1) ignore the behavior or

2) give an immediate consequence.

Ignoring the behavior doesn't get the student back on task, and therefore the student isn't participating or learning.

Giving a consequence in many cases is an overreaction to a simple lapse of attention.

Here's what you *do* want to do:
Gently, and with caring guidance, give the student an opportunity to get back on task.

It's Your Turn

The Assertive Discipline Cue Cards on pages 103-106, contain four techniques that will help you redirect a student's non-disruptive off-task behavior *while you teach*. Read each technique and imagine how you can use it throughout the day to nudge students back into your lessons. Reproduce these Cue Cards, laminate them, and keep them nearby for easy and frequent review.

1 The Look

2 Physical Proximity

3 Mention Name

4 Proximity Praise

Once a student is back on track?

As soon as a student is back on task, take advantage of the opportunity to praise his or her behavior. Let the student know that paying attention in class earns positive recognition.

How often do you redirect?
How many times should you redirect students before you start giving consequences? Obviously you can't go on redirecting a student over and over within a day. At some point you may have to turn to consequences.

Here's a rule of thumb:
When you find yourself having to redirect a student three times a day you can assume that the student is not receiving enough structure to help him control his behavior. In these situations, turn to your disciplinary hierarchy and issue a warning.

If the off-task behavior still continues, you may need to proceed further and use consequences from your disciplinary hierarchy.

Note: If the off-task behavior seems out of character for a student, perhaps there's something wrong. Before turning to consequences, talk to the student and ask, for example, "It seems like it's hard for you to pay attention in class today. Would you like to talk about it?" Always remember that your own good judgment is your most valuable guide in assessing student behavior.

ASSERTIVE
DISCIPLINE
in Action!

The "Look"

Just giving a look that says, "I'm aware of and disapprove of your behavior" is an effective way of redirecting non-disruptive off-task behavior.

Here's how this technique works:

Instead of reading her book, Jessica sits rocking back and forth in her seat. When the teacher notices Jessica's off-task behavior, she makes direct eye contact with her and looks at her with a firm, calm look on her face. She maintains this eye contact until Jessica puts all four legs of her chair on the floor and begins reading her book.

CUE CARD # 5

ASSERTIVE
DISCIPLINE
in Action!

Physical Proximity

Sometimes you don't even have to say a word to redirect a student back on task. Simply walk over and stand close by the student. The student will know why you've arrived at his or her side and will respond.

Here's an example of physical proximity at work:

While reading a story to the class, the teacher notices that Danny has put his head down on his desk and has "tuned out." Continuing to read, the teacher walks back to Danny's desk and stands near his desk while she proceeds with the story. Danny notices her presence, lifts his head and starts paying attention.

CUE CARD # 6

ASSERTIVE
DISCIPLINE
in Action!

Mention the off-task student's name while teaching.

Just mentioning a student's name while you are teaching a lesson may be enough to redirect his or her attention back on task.

Here's an example of a teacher using this technique:

While at the board, the teacher notices that Rosa and Michael are off task and not paying attention. The teacher, in a matter-of-fact manner, continues the lesson saying, "I want all of you, including Rosa and Michael, to come up with the answer to this problem." As soon as their names are mentioned, Rosa and Michael immediately begin paying attention.

CUE CARD # 7

ASSERTIVE
DISCIPLINE
in Action!

Proximity Praise

An effective way to redirect a non-disruptive off-task student back on task is to focus on the appropriate *behavior of those students around him.*

Here's an example of a teacher using proximity praise:

The entire class, with the exception of Jason, is working independently on their assignments. Rather than doing his assignment, Jason is idly doodling pictures in his notebook. On either side of Jason, Colleen and Jeff are both doing their work. Wanting to get Jason on task, the teacher says, "Colleen and Jeff are doing an excellent job on their assignments."

As she expects, Jason looks around him, notices what is going on and gets back to work.

This technique is doubly effective. Off-task students are motivated to get back on task, and students who are on task receive well-deserved praise.

CUE CARD # 8

Implementing Consequences

Students need to learn that negative consequences are a natural outcome of misbehavior. When students disrupt and keep you from teaching, or other students from learning, you will have to follow through with consequences.

On page 44 you learned to develop a discipline hierarchy as part of your classroom discipline plan. How you use the consequences in the hierarchy will determine its success in helping you motivate students to choose responsible behavior.

> Remember: The key is not the consequences themselves, but the inevitability that they will occur each time a rule is broken or a direction is not followed. Not sometimes. Not every now and then, but every single time.

Students will not respect your praise unless it is backed up with firm limits, and limits will be ineffective unless staying within those limits is backed up by praise.

Follow these guidelines to ensure that your use of disciplinary consequences will help students choose responsible behavior.

1. Provide consequences in a calm, matter-of-fact manner.

One of the benefits of a discipline hierarchy is that you always know how you will react to student misbehavior. Because you've *planned* how to deal with misbehavior, you will be able to give consequences calmly, without anger and with the assuredness that the consequence is both appropriate and fair.

"Beverly, this is the second time I've had to speak to you about running in the classroom. You have chosen to go to the time-out area for five minutes."

2. Be consistent. Provide a consequence every time a student chooses to disrupt.

As we have pointed out, it is the consistency of consequences that is the key to their effectiveness.

3. After a student receives a consequence, find the first opportunity you can to recognize positive behavior.

After a consequence has been given, teachers often continue to focus on that student's negative behavior—just waiting for the student to "act up" again. This may be a natural response, but it does little to encourage a student to choose more appropriate behavior.

Don't look for negative behavior. Instead, take the first opportunity to recognize the student's appropriate behavior.

4. Provide an "escape mechanism" for students who are upset and want to talk about what happened.

After receiving a consequence, students will often want you to stop what you are doing and listen to their side of the story.

The following "escape mechanisms" will let students diffuse their anger and "get something off their chest," without disrupting the rest of the class:

- Have the student write you a note that you will discuss with him or her after class or when you have a break in the lesson.
- Use a notebook to record misbehavior that allows space for students to write their comments.
- Have students keep a daily journal or diary in which they can record any comments.

5. When a student continuously disrupts, "move in."

There may be times when a student will continue to disrupt even after he or she has been given a warning or a consequence. In these situations, a technique called "moving in" (see Cue Card #9 on the next page) will often effectively stop disruptive behavior.

Keep in mind that by providing consequences calmly and consistently, you will effectively help most students choose responsible behavior, and stop most disruptive behavior in your classroom. In spite of these efforts, however, there are going to be some cases in which students will challenge your authority and confront you. When a student tries to manipulate you or argue with you, you must stay in charge and refocus the conversation. Refer to the refocusing technique on Cue Card #10 (page 110) for specific guidelines.

Refer to pages 169-186 of the revised Assertive Discipline text for sample scenarios demonstrating teachers effectively using consequences in a variety of teaching situations.

ASSERTIVE
DISCIPLINE
in Action!

"Moving In"

Many times physical proximity is all that is needed to help calm down a student and stop the disruptive behavior. Here's an effective technique to use when a student is being disruptive in class:

1 **Move close to the student.**

Walk over to the student. Get close. Show your concern and in a quiet, firm manner let the student know that his or her behavior is inappropriate.

2 **In a caring manner, remind the student of the consequences received so far, and what will happen next if the misbehavior continues.**

"Monica, I am concerned that your behavior today is going to result in consequences that you don't really want. You've been doing such a good job all week. I'm proud of the work you've done and I'd like to see it continue. Now you've received a warning and two consequences. One more disruption and I will be calling your parents tonight. Do you understand?"

CUE CARD # 9

ASSERTIVE
DISCIPLINE
in Action!

Refocusing an argumentative conversation

When a student starts arguing with you, you must stay in charge. Do not get involved in an argument. Do not let the student pull you into a pointless exchange. Instead, stay in control, refocus the conversation and help get the student back on task.

Here's what to do:

- Stay calm.
- State what you want: "I want you to sit down and do your assignment."
- Preface your statement of want with understanding for the child.
- Repeat your statement of want a maximum of three times. If the student still argues, let her know that she may be choosing to receive a consequence.

Here's an example of a teacher using the refocusing technique with a disruptive student:

Teacher: (*calmly but firmly*) Janis, I want you to sit down and get to work on your assignment.

Janis: Why do *I* always have to sit down? Katy gets to clean up the reading area. That's not fair.

Teacher: I understand, Janis, but I want you to sit down and start your work.

Janis: But I want to help Katy put away books. I don't want to sit down.

Teacher: Janis, I see that you're upset, but sit down and begin your work.

Janis: Everyone else always gets to help.

Teacher: Janis, if you do not get to work immediately, you and I will call your mother during recess. The choice is yours.

CUE CARD # 10

SECTION FOUR

Difficult Students

Consistent use of the classroom management skills presented in the first part of this workbook will enable most teachers to teach 90-95% of their students to choose responsible behavior.

The remaining 5-10%—the difficult students you sometimes encounter—are the focus of this section, in which we will cover four aspects of dealing successfully with difficult students:

- One-to-One Problem-Solving Conferences
- Using Positive Support to Build Positive Relationships
- Developing an Individualized Behavior Plan
- Getting Support from Parents and Administrators

One-to-One Problem-Solving Conferences

A one-to-one problem-solving conference is a meeting between you and your student to discuss a specific behavior problem. The goal of this conference is not to punish but to listen to the student and give caring and firm guidance. This conference should be looked upon as a cooperative effort on the student's behalf.

How do you know when a one-to-one conference is needed?

Ask yourself, "If this were my child, would I want her teacher to sit down and work with her to help improve her behavior? Would I want her teacher to take the time and interest to show my child better options?"

If the answer is yes, then it is time to meet with the student.

Keep these guidelines in mind when conducting a one-to-one problem-solving conference:

1. Show empathy and concern.
First and foremost, let the student know that you are concerned and that you care about him or her. Let the student know that you are meeting not to punish but to help and offer guidance.

2. Question the student to find out why there is a problem.
Don't assume you know why the student is misbehaving. Ask questions.

> "Did something happen today to get you so upset?"
>
> "Are other students bothering you?"
>
> "Do you have trouble seeing the board?"
>
> "Is the work too difficult for you?"
>
> "Is there something happening at home or in your neighborhood that's causing problems?"

3. Determine what you can do to help.
Is there anything you can do to help solve the problem? There may in fact be a simple answer that you don't want to overlook.

For example:

- If a student is having trouble in class with another student, move his seat.
- If a disruptive student is seated at the back of the class, consider moving her forward.
- Contact the parents if you feel the student needs additional help and support from home.
- Increase your positive attention toward the student, not just your consequences. Look for the first praiseworthy behavior after the conference, then send a positive note or behavior award home.
- A student may need academic help that you, a tutor or a peer study buddy may be able to provide. Make that help available.

4. Determine how the student can improve his behavior.
Ask the student for his or her input concerning ways to improve the problem behavior. Share ideas. Keep in mind that some students may not be willing or unable to share their feelings about choosing different behavior. If this is the case, help them by pointing out more appropriate behavior.

5. Agree on a course of action.
Combine your input with the student's input and agree upon a plan of action both of you can follow to improve the situation.

6. Clearly state to the student that you expect him to change his behavior.

At some point during the conference you must let the student know that you expect behavior to improve.

> "I'm going to work with you to solve this problem, Leslie. You're a smart student and I know you can behave responsibly. But you have to remember that fighting is not allowed at our school. Anytime you fight you will be choosing to go to the principal."

7. Summarize the conference. Show your confidence!

Wrap up the conference by summarizing what was said. Most important, end with a note of confidence.

> "I think we made a good start today. I know you can do better. Starting tomorrow, it will be different. I'm glad we had this talk."

Grades K-3

Young students are very concrete. Your discussion must be very specific about how the child should behave. You may actually want to roleplay the behaviors you want the student to engage in to ensure that he or she understands what you mean.

Grades 4-6

At this age students do not want to be told what to do. They want to feel they have a say in how they choose to behave. Whenever possible, involve the student in discussing how he or she should change behavior.

Refer to pages 207-216 of the revised Assertive Discipline text for examples of scripted one-to-one problem-solving conferences.

It's Your Turn

Use the Problem-Solving Conference Worksheet on page 114 as a guide for conducting the conference and as a record of what was accomplished at the conference. If parents need to be involved at a future date, you will have documentation of steps already taken to solve the problem.

PROBLEM-SOLVING CONFERENCE
WORKSHEET

Student's name ______________________ Date__________

1. Problem behavior the student is having (reason for conference):

2. Student input regarding problem (Why does the student think this problem is occurring?):

3. Steps the teacher can take to help solve the problem:

4. Actions the student can take to solve the problem:

5. Course of action agreed upon between teacher and student:

Follow-up and Notes:

114 Assertive Discipline Elementary Workbook © 1992 Lee Canter & Associates

PROBLEM-SOLVING CONFERENCE
WORKSHEET

Student's name ______________________________ Date______________

1. Problem behavior the student is having (reason for conference):

____

____

____

2. Student input regarding problem (Why does the student think this problem is occurring?):

____

____

3. Steps the teacher can take to help solve the problem:

____

____

____

4. Actions the student can take to solve the problem:

____

____

____

5. Course of action agreed upon between teacher and student:

____

____

____

____

____

Follow-up and Notes:

____

____

____

____

____

____

Using Positive Support to Build Positive Relationships

Make a special effort to establish positive relationships with difficult students—relationships that demonstrate your care and commitment to their success and well being. Show these students that you care about them as unique individuals and that you are deeply concerned about their behavior.

In order to successfully raise the self-esteem of a difficult student, you may have to go beyond your daily program of praise and positive reinforcement. Use special approaches and activities that enable you to reach out to those students on an individual basis to build a strong, positive relationship.

It's as simple as this: Treat students the way you would want your own child to be treated in school.

It's Your Turn

The following pages contain ideas for fostering and building positive relationships with difficult students—Student Interest Inventory, Teacher Interest Inventory and an Assertive Discipline Cue Card detailing effective techniques to use with difficult students.

Discover Your Students' Interests

In order to establish personal relationships with your students, you need to learn about their likes and dislikes, interests and goals. A Student Interest Inventory, taken at the beginning of the year, is a great way to learn more about each student. Explain to your students that this inventory will help you become better acquainted with each student. Make this inventory (page 116) the first homework assignment of the year. Keep a supply of Student Interest Inventories on hand throughout the year to give to transfer students entering your classroom. The information you gather from this inventory could be the building blocks of a positive student/teacher relationship.

Turnabout is fair play!

Don't forget, students will want to know something about you, too. Create a Teacher Interest Inventory detailing your likes and dislikes, interests and goals. Distribute a copy of the completed inventory to each student. Encourage students to discuss the inventory with you. Use the reproducible on page 117. (For younger students, share this information orally, followed by a question-and-answer period.)

Ideas for Building Positive Relationships

Build strong, positive relationships with difficult students by incorporating the simple, yet effective techniques found on Assertive Discipline Cue Card #11 into your daily routine. Keep this cue card handy as a reminder of the many ways you can make positive contact with all students, especially difficult ones, throughout the day.

Refer to pages 217-226 of the revised Assertive Discipline text for additional suggestions for building positive relationships with students.

STUDENT INTEREST INVENTORY

Name ______________________________

Adults who live with me:

Name______________________________

Name______________________________

Name______________________________

Name______________________________

Brothers and Sisters

Name ______________________ Age__________

Name ______________________ Age__________

Name ______________________ Age__________

Name ______________________ Age__________

Special friends: ______________ ______________

______________ ______________

What I like to do most at home: ______________________

____

These are my favorite hobbies: ______________________

____

This is my favorite book: ______________________

This is my favorite TV show: ______________________

This is my favorite movie: ______________________

If I had one wish, I would want to: ______________________

____

School would be better if: ______________________

____

If I had a million dollars, I would: ______________________

____

This is what my teacher did last year that I liked the most: ______________

____

____

This is what my teacher did last year that I liked the least: ______________

____

TEACHER INTEREST INVENTORY

Name ____

Family (optional):

Spouse ____

Children (ages) ____

Brothers and sisters? ____

What I like to do most at home: ____

____

____

These are my favorite hobbies: ____

____

____

This is my favorite book: ____

This is my favorite TV show: ____

This is my favorite movie: ____

This is my favorite performer: ____

If I had one wish, I would want to: ____

____

____

If I had a million dollars, I would: ____

____

____

What I like best about teaching: ____

____

____

Why I became a teacher: ____

____

____

____

____

ASSERTIVE
DISCIPLINE
in Action!

Ideas for Using Positive Support to Build Positive Relationships

• Greet your students at the door.

Start each day with a smile and a personal greeting—for each and every student. Stand at the door as your students enter the room and greet each student by name. "Good morning, Johnny. Nice to see you, Sally. Hi, Jeff." This is an especially effective way to make personal, positive contact with those students who need your individual attention and caring words.

• Spend a few special minutes with students who need your one-to-one attention.

The most precious and valuable gift you can give difficult students is your undivided attention. Take a few minutes during class, at recess, during lunch or after school to talk with the student. Share information about yourself. Inquire about the student's feelings and concerns. Let that student know that you are there to offer assistance, understanding and a sympathetic ear when necessary.

• Make home visits.

One very effective way to gain insight into a difficult student's behavior is to visit that student and his or her family at their home. Getting acquainted on this neutral ground is a great way to build positive relationships with difficult students and their families. Prearrange a home visit with the family. At the meeting inquire about their concerns and goals for the school year. Share your plans.

• Make a phone call after a difficult day.

End a difficult day on a positive note by phoning a student with a positive message about tomorrow. Discuss any difficulties that occurred during the day. Get student input. Most important, your phone call should emphasize your confidence that these problems can be worked through and that tomorrow both of you can start fresh.

• Make a positive phone call when a student has had a good day.

What better way to let a student know that he or she is on the right track than by making a quick phone call to offer some well-earned words of praise. If the student isn't home, share the good news with parents and have them deliver the positive message later.

• Make get-well calls.

When a student is ill, pick up the phone and call to find out how the child is feeling. Both parents and student will appreciate your caring and concern.

CUE CARD # 11

Developing an Individualized Behavior Plan

When your general classroom discipline plan is not effective with a student, you'll need to establish an individualized behavior plan for him or her. Such a plan is designed to adapt the concepts of your regular classroom discipline plan to meet the unique needs of a particular student.

An individualized behavior plan can help teach the student to behave responsibly and help you to develop the positive relationship with that student that so far may have been out of reach.

An individualized behavior plan includes:

- The specific behaviors expected of the student.
- Meaningful consequences to be imposed if the student does not choose to engage in the appropriate behavior.
- Meaningful positive recognition to be given when the student does behave appropriately.

Guidelines for developing an individualized behavior plan:

1. Determine the behavior(s) you expect from the student.

Select one or two behaviors to work on at a time. Choose those that you believe are most important to the student's success. For example, if a student has a consistent problem with staying in his seat, the rule "Stay in your seat unless told to get up" would be an appropriate behavior to target.

2. Decide on meaningful consequences.

Often you will find that a difficult student reaches the same consequence on the discipline hierarchy each day. For example, a student might reach the third step on the hierarchy every day and stay after class for two minutes on each of those days.

First disruption:	Warning
Second disruption:	One minute after class
Third disruption:	**Two minutes after class**
Fourth disruption:	Contact parents
Fifth disruption:	Send student to principal

Conclusion? It appears in this case that the student does not really mind staying after class and thus the consequence is not effective.

If you look at it in another way, you will note that the student *always* stops short of the consequence that involves calling the parent. In this case the teacher can conclude that it may be effective to individualize this student's discipline plan so that the first time she disrupts, instead of a warning or staying after class, her parents are immediately contacted.

First disruption:	Call parents
Second disruption:	Send student to principal

Note: It may be appropriate with some difficult students to provide consequences that are not on your classroom discipline hierarchy. It may be necessary, for example, to keep a student in at recess or lunch even though those consequences are not on your hierarchy.

Keep in mind that no matter what the consequence is, it must always be one that will be meaningful to the student and, as always, provided consistently each time the student chooses to misbehave.

3. Determine more meaningful positive recognition.

Your firmer, more meaningful consequences must always be balanced with increased positive recognition. As always, your positive recognition should begin with praise. Once you have implemented an individualized behavior plan, look for every opportunity to recognize the student's appropriate behavior. Make it a point to praise the student several times a day.

Back up your praise with other forms of positive recognition that you feel are appropriate, such as positive notes home or special privileges.

It's Your Turn

Use the Individualized Behavior Plan form on page 121 to help prepare and record a student's individualized plan.

The individualized behavior plan should be presented to the student in a firm but emphatic manner. Difficult students need your assurance that you care, that you are there to help and that the disruptive behavior is not in their best interests.

Refer to pages 233-234 of the revised Assertive Discipline text for a sample script for presenting an individualized behavior plan to a student.

INDIVIDUALIZED BEHAVIOR PLAN

Student's name ______________________ Date ________

These are the rule that ______________ is expected to follow as part of this Individualized Behavior Plan:

____

____

____

These are the consequences ______________ will choose to receive if he/she does not comply with the rule(s):

First disruption: ______________________

Second disruption: ____________________

This is the positive recognition ______________ will receive when he/she behaves appropriately.

____

____

____

____

____

Teacher's signature   Date

Notes or comments:

____

____

____

____

____

____

____

____

____

____

© 1992 Lee Canter & Associates   121

INDIVIDUALIZED BEHAVIOR PLAN

Student's name ____ Date __________

These are the rules that ______________________ is expected to follow as part of this Individualized Behavior Plan:

____

____

____

These are the consequences ______________________ will choose to receive if he/she does not comply with the rule(s):

First disruption: ____

Second disruption: ____

This is the positive recognition ______________________ will receive when he/she behaves appropriately.

____

____

____

____

____

Teacher's signature Date

Notes or comments:

____

____

____

____

____

____

____

____

____

____

Getting the Support You Need from Parents and Administrators

In Section 1 you learned the importance of sharing your discipline plan with parents and with your administrator. These are important proactive measures that will help ensure that you get their support when you need it.

Keep these additional guidelines in mind as the year progresses and as behavior problems arise:

When a problem arises, take steps to deal with it on your own before asking for help.

Whenever appropriate, you should attempt to handle a student's disruptive behavior on your own before you speak to the parents or administrator about the situation. Both will want to know what actions you have taken to help the student. Assure them that you have already attempted to solve the problem on your own.

Remember, your goal is to teach the student to make good behavioral choices. If you involve parents or the administrator too soon, you are not allowing the student the opportunity to change his or her own behavior.

Document a student's behavior, and the steps you have taken to handle it.

When and if you do contact parents or an administrator about a problem, you will need accurate anecdotal documentation detailing when the problem has occurred and what steps you have taken to deal with it. Documentation strengthens your position as a professional and communicates clearly to parents that these problems do exist.

Your anecdotal record should include the following information:

- Student's name
- Date, time and place of incident
- Description of the problem
- Actions taken by the teacher.

For example:

> Name: Jonathan Smith
>
> Date: 4/24/92
>
> Problem: During math, Jonathan twice pushed Kerry's book on the floor.
>
> Actions taken: Moved Jonathan to the front of the classroom for the period.

Keep these guidelines in mind when documenting problems:

Be specific. Keep away from vague opinions. Your statements should be based on factual, observable data.

Be consistent. Document problems each time they occur. Repeated occurrences may show a pattern and be helpful in solving the problem.

It's Your Turn

Use the reproducible documentation cards on page 123 to record anecdotal data about a student's behavior. Consider duplicating the cards on index stock for added durability. Fold in half with name facing forward.

Behavior Documentation Cards

Student ____________________ Phone # ____________

Parent's Name ______________ Work # ____________

Parent's Name ______________ Work # ____________

•Date ________ Time ________ Place ____________

Description of Problem/Incident: ____________________

____

Action Taken: ______________________________

____

•Date ________ Time ________ Place ____________

Description of Problem/Incident: ____________________

____

Action Taken: ______________________________

____

•Date ________ Time ________ Place ____________

Description of Problem/Incident: ____________________

____

Action Taken: ______________________________

____

•Date ________ Time ________ Place ____________

Description of Problem/Incident: ____________________

____

Action Taken: ______________________________

____

Student ____________________ Phone # ____________

Parent's Name ______________ Work # ____________

Parent's Name ______________ Work # ____________

•Date ________ Time ________ Place ____________

Description of Problem/Incident: ____________________

____

Action Taken: ______________________________

____

•Date ________ Time ________ Place ____________

Description of Problem/Incident: ____________________

____

<fold here>

Action Taken: ______________________________

____

•Date ________ Time ________ Place ____________

Description of Problem/Incident: ____________________

____

Action Taken: ______________________________

____

•Date ________ Time ________ Place ____________

Description of Problem/Incident: ____________________

____

Action Taken: ______________________________

____

Getting Support from Parents When a Problem Arises

How do you know when you should contact a parent about a problem? Some situations are very clear: severe fighting, extreme emotional distress, a student who refuses to work or turn in homework. Don't think twice about involving parents when these situations occur.

What about the day to day instances that may not be so obvious? If you are uncertain about contacting a parent, use the "Your Own Child" test. This test will put you in the position of the parent, and help clarify whether or not parental help is called for.

The "Your Own Child" Test

1. Assume you have a child of your own the same age as the student in question.
2. If your child was having the same problem in school as that student has, would you want to be called?
3. If the answer is yes, call the parent. If the answer is no, do not call the parent.

Before you pick up a phone or meet with parents, you need to outline what you are going to say. These notes will help you think through and clarify the points you want to make. Having the notes in front of you while you're speaking will help you communicate more effectively.

It's Your Turn

Assertive Discipline Cue Card #12 lists all the points you'll want to cover when contacting a parent about a problem. Reproduce and laminate this Cue Card and keep it available for use. Use the reproducible planning sheet on page 126 to help both prepare for your meeting and to record pertinent data from the meeting.

ASSERTIVE
DISCIPLINE
in Action!

Contacting Parents About a Problem

Follow these steps when contacting a parent about a problem:

1 Begin with a statement of concern.

Let the parent know that you care about the student .

2 Describe the specific problem and present pertinent documentation.

Explain in specific, observable terms what the student did.

3 Describe what you have done.

Explain exactly how you have dealt with the problem so far. Make sure that the parent is aware of the steps you have already taken to solve the problem.

4 Get parental input on the problem.

Listen carefully to what the parent has to say. Here are some questions you may want to ask:

"Has your child had similar problems in the past?"

"Why do you feel your child is having these problems at school?"

"Is there something (divorce, separation, siblings, a move) going on at home that could be affecting your child's behavior?"

5 Get parental input on how to solve the problem.

Parents may have a good idea that could help solve a specific problem. Ask for input, and listen carefully to the responses.

6 Tell the parent what you will do to help solve the problem.

You've already explained what you have previously done. Let the parent know exactly what specific actions you are going to take now.

7 Explain what you need the parent to do to solve the problem.

Clearly and carefully explain specifically what you would like the parent to do.

8 Let the parent know you are confident that the problem can be worked out.

Wrap up the conversation or meeting on a positive note.

9 Tell the parent that there will be follow-up contact from you.

The parent needs to know that you are going to stay involved. Provide this reassurance by giving a specific date for a follow-up call or note.

10 Recap the conference.

Clarify all agreements. Restate and write down what you are going to do and what the parent is going to do. Keep this information in your files.

CUE CARD # 12

PARENT CONTACT WORKSHEET

Guidelines for an initial phone call or conversation about a problem

Student's name ______________________ Date of call or meeting ______________________

Parent or guardian ____

Home phone # ______________________ Work phone # ______________________

In the spaces below write the important points you will cover with the parents, and points made during the meeting or conversation.

1. Begin with a statement of concern. ____

____

2. Describe the specific problem (state in observable terms). ______________________

____

3. Review what you have already done to solve the problem. ______________________

____

4. Get parental input on how to solve the problem. Record parent comments. ______________________

____

5. Present your solutions to the problem.

What you will do: ____

____

What you want the parent to do: ____

____

6. Express confidence once again in your ability to solve the problem.

7. Arrange for follow-up contact.

Notes ____

____

____

NOTES:

NOTES: